True Profitability

PEDRO FERRO

&

PATRICK MOSIMANN

CONTENTS

FOREWORD

This book is the third in a series addressing business complexity. I suppose this obsession originated from our long professional careers, where we've come to experience firsthand the damaging effects that unmanaged complexity has on the company's performance. Not only we've seen it destroy profitability, but we can attest to the fact that it made life miserable for everyone in the organization. It had people working overtime on petty initiatives and projects that did not matter much to the company's success. In a few instances, it led to plain and simple destruction of the firm.

In most cases, complexity was self-inflicted when executives decided to undertake growth at any cost — botched acquisitions, unsuccessful products, loss-making customers, and above all, a laisse-fare attitude towards simplification in general. A risky mindset which accepts that "all business is good business." Growth at any cost, no matter how. For the most part, managers were incapable of defining complexity to the organization, let alone measure its impact.

However, unlike the previous books, this one is not entirely about simplification, but rather about how companies can use "controlled complexity" to their advantage and enlarge their product and customer portfolios while remaining profitable. We call these companies "masters of complexity." They can define and separate beneficial from detrimental complexity and, for the most part, control the direct consequences of both forms. An example of valuable complexity is when businesses offer vast numbers of products, sometimes in the millions, to attract new customers. These companies have a way to push diversification and growth to the limit and still avoid chaos. They have a method to their madness. This book is about our observations about their approaches and how they use product variety and customer diversification to grow true profitability.

True profitability is the real measure of a company's economic success. It's pure profit devoid of arbitrary allocations or interpretations created by conventional accounting systems. It starts with the contribution margin and ends with the free cash generated by the combination of products and customers. It's money in the pocket. Moreover, contribution margin is a better metric to start with, as it represents a clean ratio between price, which is defined by the market, and direct cost, which is achieved by the company's abilities and skills. It's the purest indicator of economic performance and value that we can find in a business. Everything else is abstraction and convention.

Masters of complexity use true profitability to steer through the chaos created by very long tails, excessive customer and vendor transactions, complicated supply chain logistics, and many other challenges. True profitability guides them to rationalize portfolios, standardize processes and products and to create modularity and simplicity in their vast offerings. They also make good use of the data they collect from the interplay of physical and virtual assets. Their online presence is an extension of their brick-and-mortar infrastructure, and not just an attempt to create a new sales channel. The data collected and the analytics used to unveil true profitability are as critical as the products and services themselves.

Considering the importance of data collection and analysis, Patrick and I have partnered here to describe how we use model-based analytics to arrive at True Profitability. Patrick is the CEO of a global data science company (AlignAlytics) and knows more about the theme than I would ever be able to explain. We have collaborated on several projects so far and have developed a unique approach to complexity analytics. The reader can access a self-evaluation tool based on our experiential analytics model by accessing a link on the internet.[i]

Notwithstanding the wild pace of change imposed by the digital transformation, one mental model remains true to reality over the years – the Pareto Principle. The larger "big-data" gets, the more useful the Pareto Principle becomes, to uncover relationships that we did not know exist in the data. Masters of complexity implant the Pareto Principle in their analytical models, using Artificial Intelligence and Machine Learning, to discover new patterns within the business, other than the archetypical 80/20 distribution - ratios like 55/1 and 45/70, for example. These extreme proportions or Super-Paretos, form the basis for a new set of KPIs or Key Pareto Indicators.

We hope that the next pages will inspire the reader to rethink complexity management and have a different understanding of product and customer profitability. By uncovering the good and the not-so-good areas of the portfolio under the lenses of true profitability, managers will be able to use more precise analytical approaches to improve performance.

True Profitability

1 MASTERS OF COMPLEXITY

The purpose of this book is to help companies make the most money from the combination of products and customers in their portfolios while curtailing harmful complexity. We are referring to maximizing the cash that remains in the business after we account for the overhead used to create and sell products and support customers. This cash is referred to as "free cash" or "pocket money." People aside, customers and products (or services), are two of the most valuable assets a business can have. Over time complexity will inevitably enter a company's portfolio and move resources from high-value to low-value activities, hurting customer satisfaction, putting pressure on profitability, and reducing free cash flow.

When earnings decrease, managers typically display one of several behaviors towards fixing the problem. The natural reaction is to ignore the issue and let the course of business get rid of loss-making customers and low-margin products. The let-it-be attitude takes a long time to work and usually requires a deep crisis to have a transformative impact. The second type of behavior is one that recognizes and defines complexity as the root cause of the problem for the organization. Managers try to fix the causes by optimizing the portfolio using pricing, product changes, and customer attrition. This conduct is more rewarding than letting-it-be. It is, however, often based on the false premise that lasting and final optimization is possible to achieve.

The other posture, which is central to digital marketing, embraces variety and accepts complexity as a fact of life. Rather than aiming for continual optimization, this mindset uses data to qualify complexity, separating the good from the bad kind. Managers recognize that variety is essential, using bounded rationality to make decisions, instead of pursuing the illusion of complete optimization. They learn how to work and prosper with a large and complex portfolio by actively governing complexity.

Bounded Rationality is a notion perfected by Herbert Simonii and states that "when individuals make decisions, their rationality is limited by the tractability of the decision problem, the cognitive limitations of their minds, and the time available to make the decision. Decision-makers act as satisficers, seeking a satisfactory solution rather than an optimal one. We satisfice rather than optimize. Decision-makers do not have to be omniscient or perfectly rational; they need only pursue decisions that prove good enough. For all the talk of optimization in boardrooms or C-suites, performing better than the competition will generally carry the day."

The last behavior is welcoming to beneficial complexity or the type of product diversity that attracts new buyers if the free cash flow justifies the cost of handling it. Customer data analytics is essential to manage an extensive offering, coupled with virtual supply chains and efficient logistics.

Variety is inherent to the consumer economy because it sells. We live in a time of abundant choice when customers expect and demand selection and assortment. It's valuable from both functional and emotional aspects. At the practical level, it satisfies concrete needs to use a product or to complement a customer's offering, in a business-to-business transaction. At an emotional level, variety caters to underlying human feelings of survival in multiple dimensions. Finding the exact products or services you need to do a job, take care of a pain point, or to appeal to your passions and desires is hugely satisfying.

Click-and-brick stores such as Walmart and Target, and pure online retailers like Amazon and Alibaba, use the endless assortment as a common tactic to attract new customers. Offering a broad range of items to entice buyers is an old formula known to marketers since the early days.

Farmers' markets, open street bazaars, and shopping malls are all examples of selling by offering variety. If you observe markets in emerging countries, you will find whole streets, squares, and multi-vendor bazaars that specialize in selling the same types of products. Side-by-side stores offering garments, electronic gadgets, street food, toys, and flowers, for example, survive and thrive together despite the competition next door. Customers are attracted to such marketplaces as they look for assortment, specialization, and the awareness that competing stores can always deliver a better deal.

The long tail

In 2004 Chris Anderson from Wired Magazine wrote a somewhat controversial article titled "The Long Tail." The basic premise of the article was that our consumer culture and economy have a growing appetite for unique products and services. To be successful and attract buyers, retailers need an ever-growing selection and variety of items to sell. The desire for specialized and niche products is continually stretching the tail of the demand curve.

The line at the bottom of the demand curve keeps getting bigger (the long tail) in comparison with the head. The article synthesized the essence of online marketplaces, where consumers are increasingly able to select products based on ever so specialized and fragmented tastes and wants. It portrayed the viability of catering to small niche markets for companies like Amazon. Chris Anderson went on to write a book on the theme in 2006, titled "The Long Tail: Why the Future of Business Is Selling Less of More."

1.1 The Long Tail

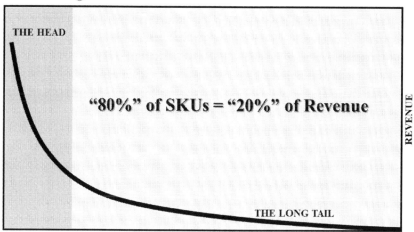

Every shopper has undoubtedly experienced the endless choice in the long tail when searching for things to buy at Amazon. Plentiful categories and variations, including oddities such as bacon-flavored dental floss and a desktop pillow for those hung-over days at the office, amongst millions of other specific articles.

Take Amazon's first major product category, books, for example. They have increased the number of titles and singular subjects to an extreme over the years. You can find books about virtually anything in their store. The demand for alternative titles has created a new marketplace for authors. Any writer today, including this one, can exist in the long tail, through self-publishing tools like Kindle's Direct Publishing. This ultra-fragmentation trend eventually spilled over other product categories prompting niche retailers and manufacturers to use Amazon's marketplace to sell their products.

Since Chris Anderson's article in 2004, there has been a lot of debate regarding the validity of the long tail as a workable business model. The controversy around the model theory is that it does not apply outside of internet retailing. The long tail in manufacturing, for example, behaves differently than the long tail in pure online selling. We find that these discussions mostly miss the point. It's fair to say that only a few internet distribution companies can afford to base most of their business in the long tail model. However, even click-only retailers, such as Amazon, do not live entirely in the long tail. Amazon uses the long tail to attract buyers with variety, making a profit when retailers sell a product through their virtual marketplace. Amazon also employs the web store to capture data, to know what buyers are clicking on and looking for online. The data is vital to decide what to stock in their warehouses and what to outsource to affiliated retailers. Approximately 7% of the items sold by Amazon are in the head of the curve, while 93% of the products are in the long tail. The clicks and customer's behavior data are critical to Amazon's success.

Furthermore, we should not think of the long tail only as a business model but as a business reality that happens to both on and offline companies. Long tails are a fact of life. When we examine the diversity of customers and products combined, we find that almost all companies have a long tail. No matter how long or short, good or bad, companies can either use it to their advantage or let it become a burden, consuming the free cash flow earned at the head of the demand curve. The fact is, every business needs a strategy to deal with the long tail.

If you are a retailer or a distributor in the US today, your biggest dilemma is whether to join or to contend with Amazon. Big box retailers like Walmart, Best Buy, and Target have no alternative other than to fight. However, smaller retailers contemplate whether they should join Amazon's marketplace or create their online stores. At the heart of the decision lies the question: Who is going to own the customer data? In most cases, retailers end up joining the marketplace while creating their online stores, with the sole purpose of accumulating data on consumer behavior.

This decision about joining an established virtual marketplace or going alone is not unique to the US. Retailers all over the world are considering the pros and cons of selling through online giants such as Alibaba, Schwarz, Flipkart, and many more. Large retailers keep going back and forth in their strategies to compete with the giants.

Most recently, Walmart enhanced its online offering by adding 35,000 new SKUs (stock-keeping units), while reducing the number of items sold in physical stores by 20%. This decision was an effort to create the equivalent of an endless-aisle online and take advantage of the long tail phenomena. It was also an attempt to fight complexity at the stores (120,000 plus SKUs carried at supercenters), and create its marketplace, attracting smaller retailers. Walmart has set up kiosks outside the physical stores to influence customers into buying online. However, the program has had mixed results, and Walmart decided to restock many of the items back at the physical stores.

Walmart is also adopting an Amazon-like strategy in emerging markets. In 2018, it announced the acquisition of 77 percent of Flipkart, India's largest online retailer, for US$16 billion. The deal was supposed to give the world's largest retailer better access to India's e-commerce market. Plus, it would help Walmart challenge Amazon's online sales in the country.

Variety is a reliable selling tool, but it's also the primary force behind demand fragmentation. If nothing else, it helps amass customer information. Customers are people, and people like selection, features, and choice. Life is an individual experience, and consumers are latching on to the possibility of buying one-of-a-kind goods, and companies are getting smarter about meeting the needs of a marketplace formed by a single customer.

This trend, however, is not exclusive to business-to-consumer commerce. Several online markets already exist in the business-to-business space. Chinese giant Alibaba, for example, is the world's largest e-commerce platform for industrial and commercial products, operating as a middleman between buyers and sellers. Business buyers also value the ability to buy smaller quantities of unique and very specialized items at competitive prices.

The tricky question is how conventional retailers and manufacturers can keep up with the level of portfolio expansion and specialization required to succeed. We know that they are not all prepared to adopt the same long tail business model used by Amazon. No matter how big or small, whether you make your own or buy finished products to resell, one of your most significant worries should be the cost of complexity to handle the different long tails imposed by the market.

The problem is exceptionally hard for manufacturers, considering the logistical and operational challenges to design, produce, and support so many products. To survive and thrive amidst the chaos that exists in the long tail, companies need to learn new tricks and embrace creative approaches to portfolio expansion, learning from data analytics and modularizing product lines to avoid detrimental complexity. It requires multiple strategies to keep the offering competitively supplied, such as outsourcing, low-cost country sourcing, manufacturing segregation, and more.

Fortunately, there are many examples of companies that have transformed themselves by learning how to use analytics to manage complexity. They have digitally changed the business, staying away from the black holes created by the retail apocalypse and manufacturing demise. Retailers such a Kohl's and Best Buy, for example, have braved the trend while Sears, Macy's and JCPenney are struggling, going out of business or closing stores as sales decline. The digitally transformed know that the long tail can be healed and used to bring about profitable growth.

With greater complexity in their offerings, retailers and distributors have significant amounts of external complexity, reflected in customer retention, logistics, sourcing, and inventory costs. On the other hand, manufacturers must worry about internal complexity and its many tentacles, such as design and engineering costs, part redundancy and supplier proliferation, logistics and manufacturing complexities, to cite a few.

With more than 650 million SKUs in Amazon's offering, Amazon is burdened by complex logistics, engaging and retaining retailers and understanding customer and market trends to the highest degree. The cost of complexity is there, but it doesn't grow as fast as the long tail. Every new SKU has only a small contribution to the cost of complexity, so they can efficiently add thousands of new products every day while keeping operating expenses under control.

For manufacturers, though, it's a different story. The slight growth of the long tail induces an extraordinary amount of complexity cost under the surface. Every additional product brings new components, manufacturing assets, people, and support costs. Complexity is not as friendly to manufacturers as it is to retailers.

As mentioned, everyone has a tail, and there is clear evidence that the variety drives revenue growth. However, there is also clear evidence that proliferation reduces value creation and profitability if not well managed. Most traditional industries that resisted portfolio expansion are now increasing variety, including European car producers, for example.

While the major brands used to carry an average of 100 to 150 car models only ten years ago, they are now offering an average of 250 to 300 models. Nowadays BMW has more brands (BMW, M, Mini), series variants, body styles (SUV, cross-over, sedan, coupe, convertible) and drivetrains (electric, hybrid, PEV) than ever. Mercedes-Benz and BMW are two of the most prolific brands in the US in terms of variants.

Manufacturers must learn how to manage the business in the complexity zone and grow the tail without significantly adding to the cost of complexity. In other words, they must balance portfolio expansion with scalability. Every new product or variant added to the portfolio has to contribute to the overall profitability or have a fundamental reason to exist. Offsetting the losers with the winners don't always work! The tolerance for freeloader products (the low profitability ones) gets challenged by the fact that companies are targeting markets of one: every product and every customer count.

To become masters of complexity and capitalize on product diversity, retailers and manufacturers must change in at least three ways. First, they need to embrace digital transformation, enhancing skills to predict customer behavior, and knowing real-time the financial impact of adding to the tail. Second, companies need to be better at new product introduction and portfolio management to measure the effect of expanding the offering, governing, and quantifying the actual cost of complexity for every transaction.

Third, companies must adapt their product lines to attain economies of scale, via the reuse of components, partnership with key suppliers, and leaner manufacturing plants. Companies have a lot to gain if they embark on a data-driven effort to rationalize, standardize, and modularize product lines.

Complexity governance leads to performance

Businesses display different abilities to manage variety and deal with its inherent complications. Some don't even recognize or measure the cost of carrying too many variants and merely react to market needs and internal problems. Others estimate the cost and attack complexity using a systematic approach. Based on how companies deal with the long tail opportunity and the costs of complexity, we can divide businesses into four categories:

1. **The cost-cutter:** Most companies are drawn into the long tail incrementally and, only when the symptoms become too burdensome, they launch an attack on complexity. These companies are good at continuously pruning the overhead associated with external complexity. This category includes those who

apply ABC (Activity Based Costing). Archetypical example: Ford.

2. **The Lean practitioner:** Some companies restructure internal processes to minimize complexity from inception. They recognize and deal with both causes and symptoms from within their four walls. These manufacturers make a great effort to standardize processes (engineering, purchasing, sales) and reduce variation (production lines, warranty) within their organization. It includes practitioners of Lean and Six Sigma. Archetypical example: Toyota.

3. **The simplifier (long tail cutters):** Companies that measure and recognize the problem with uncontrolled complexity. They work hard to contain product and customer variety and are always pruning the long tail and segmenting the business for increased focus on the vital few customers and products. It includes many users of the 80/20 business process. Archetypical example: ITW.

4. **The master of complexity (long tail managers):** Complexity governance is at the core of these businesses. They are savvy users of big data analytics. They embrace product variety and expansion by partnering with other vendors and channel players to

create unique offerings and develop efficient commercial ecosystems. They use true product profitability or the individual product P&L as a guide to expand the offering. Archetypical example: Amazon.

The first two types (cost-cutter and Lean practitioner) focus on the symptoms of complexity, while the third type (simplifier) centers on the causes of complexity. The fourth category (master of complexity) is concerned with creating profitable variety and distinguishing between detrimental and beneficial complexity. They are the prototypical long tail professionals and not limited to online retailers at all.

We call masters of complexity many manufacturers that have developed modular product line architectures to create profitable variety, including Scania, Rexroth, Seiko, and many others. The toy company, LEGO, has become a synonym for good assortment and modularity. When referring to Scania, for example, we can say that they use a "LEGO approach" to build and sell trucks.

Furthermore, if we look at value creation to shareholders under the lens of stock price appreciation for the four archetypical companies, we can see a significant difference amongst them. For five years alone (October/2014 to October/2018), using the SP500 index as a comparison basis, Ford and Toyota underperformed the index by 16% and 10% respectively while ITW and Amazon outperformed the SP500 by 60% and 392% respectively.

1.2 Complexity Approach Impacts Performance

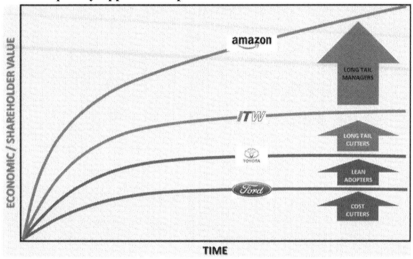

This comparison may not be entirely fair since these are different industries and market structures, but it helps illustrate the performance delta that simplifiers and masters of complexity can achieve over time. Profitable variety is a significant contributor to growth and value creation.

ITW manages the long tail by segmenting businesses continuously and having them managed by market-focused business units. Segmentation is essential because each ITW business unit has unique demand curve characteristics. For instance, for any business unit, the head of the curve may represent a lot more than 7% of total revenues, like in Amazon's case. Additionally, the long tail may not be as valuable as it appeared to be before segmentation, once managers consider all the costs associated with the tail alone.

Amazon creates variety to attract more buyers and vendors every day, offering a highly visible and desirable online marketplace to transact. The company has minimal operating costs to be divided across the millions of products living in the long tail. It's the ultimate scalability model. The long tail of the demand curve is profitable for Amazon, while the head of the curve is hugely profitable.

Scania, the Swedish truck maker, also uses product diversification to give customers options. It allows Scania to sell trucks into low-volume applications, such as logging and mining. The long tail for Scania consists of products that use similar components to high-volume truck models that are in the head of the curve, albeit assembled in unique ways. The cost of complexity is under control because of Scania's modular product line architecture.

Modular architectures and vehicle platforms are enticing to automotive companies. Recently, Ford has accelerated its efforts to simplify. In 2018 it announced that it would revamp its North American product line by dropping most low-volume sedans while focusing on pick-up trucks and SUVs. While they are not changing their product line architecture yet, this is a positive step towards dealing with the causes of internal complexity.

Toyota has also embarked on a program to consolidate all its car models in 2012, down to three vehicle platforms, known as Toyota New Global Architecture (TGNA). The new architecture will increase the sharing of components among vehicles and reduce the number of models by 2020. The modular assembly program will reduce costs in several ways and will be more LEGO-like. The introduction of smaller manufacturing lines, for instance, is expected to decrease initial plant investment by approximately 40% compared with 2008 levels. Toyota is starting to tackle external complexity and going the way of simplifier companies.

Besides governing complexity and creating smart variety, simplifiers, and masters of complexity use data in unique ways. They go beyond reporting and financial analysis, with unique model-based analytical tools using the Pareto Principle as a framework to develop insight and value from big data. The inexorability of imbalances in the numbers and the clear separation between vital few and trivial many are forcing algorithms to learn and to incorporate this familiar experiential model. Time after time, big data analytics keeps pointing to the fact that only a few customers and products create most margin dollars and growth.

Data analytics, coupled with Pareto thinking, enables masters of complexity to work comfortably in the long tail. They correlate and integrate different structured and unstructured data sets to transform data into valuable insight, helping achieve the trade-off between variety and scalability. Granular insight leads to better management of individual products and customers, accounting for all the support costs involved.

In the next chapters of this book, we will try to provide a practical approach to applying the concepts of bounded rationality and Pareto Principle to the long tail. These methods should help improve the thinking, the data analysis, and the evolution towards becoming a master of complexity.

2 TRUE PROFITABILITY

The key reason why so many companies don't profit from the long tail is that they fail to define, measure, and control complexity. Managers rarely know the pocket money they get to keep (or let go) when they sell a product or a service. They only see the contribution or gross margin earned, but seldom understand the final profit or loss from every product or transaction. Monthly income statements deliver consolidated business financials, but they do not help to make decisions related to individual SKUs.

General accounting is intended to focus on production and distribution costs. It's not designed to give you the ability to manage complexity or recognize the portion of complexity costs created by each product or service. For the most part, standard accounting collects all the overhead into one or more P&L buckets, since it cannot differentiate or apportion the actual amount of cost to each product. All it can do is to allocate some of the expenses based on pre-defined rules or standards.

When allocating indirect cost, accounting systems use canned parameters based on variables associated with each product, such as revenue or another distinguishable production input like energy consumption. These allocation factors are estimates and carry high margins of error when compared to more hands-on methods, such as value stream mapping and activity-based costing (ABC). The limited accuracy has turned managers into skeptics and not very keen to support a KPI that measures the final and total profitability of a sales transaction. The debate on cost allocation accuracy to products and business units goes on forever inside many organizations. However, the reality is that conventional accounting cannot accurately measure true product profitability, and managers can make mistakes when using these figures to make decisions.

In the ideal world, working exclusively with gross margins would be acceptable. A business devoid of any complexity would manufacture and sell products with zero overhead. Companies would not need to spend money on sales or marketing. No accounting, engineering, or human resources department expenses either. The only costs would be those tied to making products, such as raw materials and labor, which vary directly with production volume. Our perfect company would have little complexity and no overhead, and all profits would flow directly to the bottom line. In this case, you can say that true product profitability is equal to the variable margin. You could use contribution margins alone to make decisions about pricing, investments, suppliers, and to decide whether you will continue to offer or eliminate a product from your portfolio.

Regrettably, many companies act as if they live in this ideal world! In reality, different products can carry very different amounts of overhead, in the form of associated support and complexity costs. Not knowing the value of indirect expenses that go with each unit can lead to some very wrong decisions, especially concerning the long tail. The real cost of highly engineered and manufactured modifications vary significantly depending on testing, sourcing, and support requirements. Even similar products can have considerably different bottom-lines, depending on production volumes, production lines, and target markets.

One can appreciate the profit imbalance among products by applying 80/20 thinking. The vast majority of items in any portfolio generate only a small amount of profit and sales dollars (the twenty percent). However, these products are also responsible for creating most of the overhead. The long tail items carry a significant amount of complexity cost. As a rule, general accounting does not capture the cost nuances between the eighty and the twenty SKUs. If the business is making money, a standard report may lead us to think that "all business is good business," as in the following example:

2.1 "All business is good business."

	TOTAL	80%	20%
REVENUES	**$1,000**	**$800**	**$200**
VARIABLE COST	**$400**	**$320**	**$80**
MATERIALS	$300	$240	$60
LABOR	$100	$80	$20
ALL OTHER COSTS	**$400**	**$320**	**$80**
INCOME	**$200**	**$160**	**$40**
	20%	20%	20%

The elements in "all other costs" are allocated based on revenue or some other criteria. However, if we were to distribute the actual cost between the eighty and the twenty, the picture would look very different, leading us to recognize why "some business is not so good." The same example would now show that the twenty percent, which represents the majority of the SKUs, are very unprofitable. The eighty, which are only a few SKUs, are more profitable than initially thought, as per the table below.

2.2 "Some business is not so good."

	TOTAL	80%	20%
REVENUES	$1,000	$800	$200
VARIABLE COST	$400	$320	$80
MATERIALS	$300	$240	$60
LABOR	$100	$80	$20
ALL OTHER COSTS	*$400*	*$80*	*$320*
INCOME	$200	$400	($200)
	20%	50%	-100%

When it comes to spreading all other costs, like ESG&A (engineering, sales & marketing, general and administrative overhead), the accounting people will have a hard time doing that. These costs remain unassociated with products since functions or departments are responsible for them. We would have to break-down each associated activity of the engineering department, for example, with a specific product during a period. The closest cost accounting methodology to do this massive task is activity-based costing or ABC.

ABC was a first attempt to apply Lean principles to accounting since it borrowed the value stream mapping concept from Lean manufacturing. According to the Chartered Institute of Management Accountants (CIMA), ABC is "an approach to the costing and monitoring of activities which involves tracing resource consumption and costing final outputs. Resources are assigned to activities and activities to cost objects based on consumption estimates. The latter utilize cost drivers to attach activity costs to outputs."

However, ABC is also very depended on estimates and is prone to inaccuracies. ABC is expensive to implement, and its data is likely to be misinterpreted. The sheer number of steps, time, and resources involved in mapping the entire portfolio of a company can be daunting, leading to shortcuts and mistakes. If applied to only a few targeted products or processes, ABC can be a useful tool for a short-lived picture but, if you have thousands of products and customers in a dynamic market environment, you may want to stay away from this method. To manage product variety, you need a more straightforward and cost-effective way to understand true profitability at the SKU level.

Defining true profitability

True profitability (TrP) is the equivalent of having an income statement for each product or service. It's the actual ability of a product to generate free cash flow and is the foundation for managing variety. If an SKU is not lucrative from a TrP standpoint, it will reduce the overall company's earnings by a certain amount. We call these products "freeloaders" since they don't carry their weight and survive thanks to other items. You can afford to have some freeloaders if you know that they will either attract new customers or sell more of your existing profitable products. In most cases, companies don't even know they have freeloaders, let alone having a conscious strategy to use them to expand profits.

Going back to Amazon, they have an insider name for freeloaders or products with low or negative true profitability. They call these items CRaP inside the company, short for "Can't Realize a Profit." Typically, CRaP is used to refer to products with thin margins that use a lot of indirect overhead, mostly warehouse space, and handling costs. Very heavy or bulky items, costly to ship, must have a higher contribution margin, to show an acceptable TrP level. For instance, packaged high-volume and low-margin goods, such as purified water or soda cases, can be considered CRaP.

The best long tail managers use data analytics to help identify freeloaders or CRaP. For most businesses, however, products are added, or allowed to continue to lose money, based on inertia or sketchy financial KPIs. A dose of commercial bias influenced by the perception that a new product is "very similar" to one that already exists is all it takes to create more freeloaders.

Despite all the discipline and structure around new product introduction, most decisions impacting the portfolio are carried on by managers without a reasonable understanding of true profitability, lacking the proper analytical tools. Typical metrics include ROI (Return on Investment) and NPV (Net Present Value), together with factors like risk-adjusted NPV and time-to-market. Problems arise when managers are forced to predict the future and make erroneous volume and margin forecasts. More projects fail to reach ROI and NPV targets because of incorrect volume and margin predictions than any other factor. Managers rely too much on questionable assumptions and too little on portfolio analytics and modeling. When a new product launch goes wrong, companies take too long to correct the problem, under the influence of the different paradigms, including the sank cost one. In the meantime, freeloaders are eating away free cash flow and operating profits.

To make proper and fast decisions, managers need a better, more practical way to arrive at the item's P&L. The best approach to measuring true profitability is to use 80/20 analytics, which is a straightforward way to allocate indirect costs (both manufacturing and ESG&A) based on the principle of imbalance for two key variables: economic value and activity.

True profitability needs "Pareto thinking."

Our collective knowledge (and the Pareto rule) tells us that twenty percent of the products (or customers) account for eighty percent of the profits. We also know by experience that the remaining products (the trivial many) are responsible for eighty percent of the complexity costs. The proportions are never precisely 80/20, but, in reality, there is always a significant imbalance between efforts and results.

The reason for this imbalance is because complexity costs increase with the levels of variety and activity. Companies typically spend way more money with the losers than they spend with the winners. Not only because they believe they will turn the losers into winners, but primarily because they don't measure the drivers of complexity. As shown, if we were to distribute the actual overhead between the eighty and twenty, using a direct cost attribution method, the picture will look very different than the one presented by general accounting, leading us to understand why some business is not so good.

As with ABC, we know that cost is directly proportional to activity and inversely proportional to economic value. As a percentage of revenues, a high-volume blockbuster product, with a substantial contribution margin, sold to a few large customers in large quantities, carries minimal complexity cost, compared to a low-volume and low-margin item sold to small customers. High-volume, high-margin products tend to evolve and become optimized over time, with fewer sub-components, fewer suppliers, better manufacturing lines, and less complexity in general.

We also know that more sales do not always mean more profits, but more transactions almost always involve more cost. Growing sales rapidly, with items which do not generate free cash flow, is not a good thing. If you are looking for leading indicators of complexity, look at revenue or transactions. They are proxies for activity, along with the part count, vendor attrition, and other effort-related metrics. Complex and labor-intensive operations will always cost more. On the other hand, simple and effortless will invariably yield lower overhead and higher economic value.

Contribution margin (CM), the result of subtracting the variable cost from the sales price, is the best proxy for economic value. It measures the amount that individual products or services contribute to net profit. The ability of a company to have a robust free cash flow from a product or service starts with sound contribution margins. There is little or nothing managers can do to improve profitability if contribution margins are negligible.

CM is used in 80/20 analytics to reveal a critical comparison that otherwise would lie hidden in the income statement - a better correlation coefficient between the market and the internal cost structure. Customers will reward value and simplicity with higher margins. On the other hand, the market will penalize complexity over time with a lower margin. A streamlined, high-value product offering will always be rewarded with more top contribution margin dollars by the market.

80/20 analytics is a better way to determine true profitability without the use of inaccurate accounting allocations and complicated methods, such as ABC. It also redeploys data from existing systems to arrive at new insights. It's not a cost accounting system but a tool to manage complexity. We can say that 80/20 analytics is a "hack" or a proxy to ABC, but it creates far more insights and benefits than ABC alone. Similar to ABC, it uses activity indicators to get at the cost of complexity and contribution margin as a surrogate to economic value.

For now, it's essential to know that activity levels and contribution margins are necessary to calculate true profitability, and we will look at the calculation method in a later chapter. Once we have the P&L for each SKU, we can start visualizing the correlation between TrP and CM under the Pareto distribution, as depicted in the next picture

2.3 True Profitability versus Contribution Margin

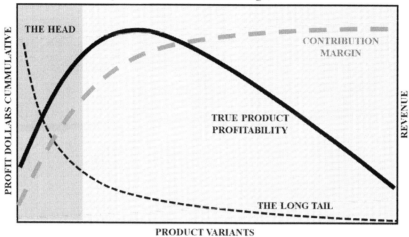

As we can see from the above, the cumulative contribution margin does not represent the ultimate profitability of the business. Only after considering the overhead impact of each SKU, we can see a more realistic picture, which is more in line with what we see in the company's P&L. The distribution of complexity costs in proportion to activity and economic value, using 80/20, allows us to realize that we have underestimated the importance of products at the head of the curve and overestimated the profitability of the ones at the long tail.

Like the cumulative contribution margin, the line that represents true profitability increases sharply in the head area of the demand curve. However, as we get closer to the tail of the portfolio, we see a sharp decline to the bottom-line, weighted down by the cost of complexity attributed to long tail products, mainly the freeloaders.

Knowing which products help or hurt the company's profitability is very important. The question then becomes: how can managers lift true profitability to reduce the gap with the contribution margin? To raise true profitability, we need to understand what is going on with each product in the context of the overall portfolio. 80/20 analytics can help create unfiltered and straightforward insight, leading to improvement actions quickly. There is no general formula. However, there is a natural path from chaos to managed complexity that we will discuss further in this book.

In the first part of this journey, managers need to challenge freeloaders or low profitability items in the portfolio. It requires data and courage to deal with the long tail inflection points. In most cases, merely phasing out or replacing products will help lift margins. In other cases, increasing prices to offset the cost of complexity will drive the improvement. As a rule, you should let the market decide if there is value in paying more to access specialty and low-volume products. Differentiated terms and conditions, channel strategies, physical separation of low-volume items are some of the typical approaches used to simplify the offering. They go way beyond just cutting the end of the tail.

Once we deal with freeloaders, we turn our attention to the items that must remain in our offering, for various reasons, but still show unsatisfactory true profitability. These are "sick products" that need healing.

Some of the same strategies used with freeloaders may apply here. Managers turn their attention to internal complexity and use standardization and optimization tactics to heal sick products. We deal with internal complexity by physically separating the production of eighty and twenty products, increasing the level of parts similarity in the bill of materials, reducing part count and optimizing direct material cost, for example. We also work on supply-base rationalization and evolve the product line architecture to become more modular. These are some examples of the types of strategies used to heal the portfolio.

Lastly, companies need a process to govern and manage the long tail, to be able to retake variety as a useful growth tool while preventing low-margin products from entering and remaining in the portfolio. Profitably growing the long tail requires engaged people and reliable information. Managers need constant and easy access to TrP to be able to separate "CraP" from winners.

3 THINKING INSIDE THE BOX

A better way to understand what is going on with your portfolio is to frame the data related to customers and products in a box. Since customers and products are linked by revenue and contribution margin, you can easily connect and organize the information according to 80/20, placing it inside of a two-by-two matrix. This simple exercise gives you a two-dimensional visualization of the demand curve, showing patterns and insights that are not always noticeable or intuitive when you look at a graph. When you associate two correlated datasets, your focus gets sharper and stronger. You also link the analysis to a defined period and a finite number of parameters, which helps expedite decisions. Pareto coupled with the Bounded Rationality[iii] principle help make sense of the data.

Where the cumulative contribution margin for customers and products reach eighty percent, that's where you draw the line between the vital few and the trivial many, creating four areas or quadrants. At the intersection of every customer and product, you enter the amounts for revenue and contribution margin for the period selected.

3.1 80/20 Customers and Products Matrix

x%................80%.......................................100%

Customers →

	Q1 *Core Products &* *Customers*	Q2 *Supporting Customers*
	Q3 *Supporting Products*	Q4 *Residual Products and Customers*

(Products axis: x% ... 80% ... 100%)

As we can see above, the most significant area is Q1, the upper left corner of the matrix. Quadrant one is where we find core products and customers (the eighty). It represents the head of the demand curve. This quad typically contains between 65% to 75% of the revenue and contribution margin, but only a small number of SKUs and buyers. It has the highest sales volume with the least amount of transactions. Typically, the products that a company sells in quad one are sourced from prime suppliers or made in highly efficient production lines. The customers are also strategic and treated with great care by separate sales and support people. Still, due to the high sales volume and supply chain effectiveness, we can say that this is the least chaotic area of the matrix.

The upper right area or quadrant two contains all other customers (the twenty). Q2 also includes data related to purchases of core products by supporting customers. It usually represents between 10% and 15% of the total revenue and contribution margin. Although customers only buy core products in this quad, this area can bring significant complexity due to the sheer number and size of transactions. Clients positioned between the 80% and 90% zones are called transitional customers and buy from the beginning of the long tail. Between 90% and 100%, we find a multitude of smaller customers, which typically buy from the tail end of the demand curve.

Quadrant three, in the lower-left corner, is where we find the ancillary or twenty products. Q3 amounts to approximately 10% to 15% of the total value and reflects the purchases of supporting products by eighty customers, typically in low volumes. Companies usually create these variants to complement a product selection intended to retain core customers. However, we also find products that are sold exclusively to twenty customers in Q4; therefore, Q3 also holds much complexity due to the proliferation of parts and suppliers. As with quadrant two, there is a transitional band of items, between 80%

and 90%, residing in the middle of the tail. Still, most SKUs live at the very end of the demand curve.

The residual area or quadrant four is the zone where we compile data related to purchases of ancillary products by supporting customers. These are usually small, low volume transactions. The data in Q4 is less dense, also known as sparse data, and tends to amalgamate or cluster in different areas of the quad. It should represent only 5% to 10% of total revenue and margin and, except for a small area on the upper left corner, most of its products are positioned at the very tail end of the demand curve. Generally, this quadrant carries the bulk of the complexity cost due to the excessive number of low volume transactions, the amount of commercial and engineering support, sourcing complexity, and support costs that are not correctly allocated.

The 80/20 customer and product matrix is a better way to visualize data patterns, anomalies, and proportions between high and low-value businesses. It contains both quantitative and qualitative data and can be divided or reduced to finer and finer levels. There is tremendous value in analyzing the matrix in conjunction with true profitability and demand curves.

When we superpose the four areas of the matrix on top of the profitability curves, as per the picture below, we see the rise and fall of true profitability across each of the quadrants. True profitability increases fast in the head of the curve, peaks around the transition zone and then starts dropping as we enter the 90% plus areas of quadrants two, three, and four. Some businesses display a sudden drop or a plunge in true profitability at the end of the curve. We call this plunge the limber-tail pattern. The severity of the fall is usually a function of the business model and how companies manage complexity.

3.2 The "limber-tail" pattern (the "plunge" in True Profitability)

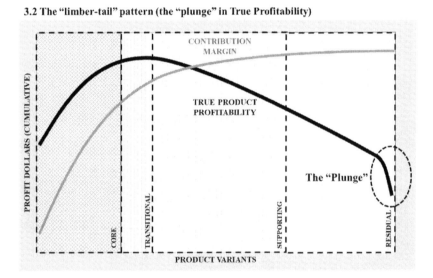

We know that most companies make most of their profits at the head of the curve and then give some (if not all) of it back as they move towards the tail end. The key questions are how much and how fast they allow true profitability to decline. The business model, for instance, the supply chain and go-to-market strategies, influence the slope and the smoothness of the curve. The complexity management dimension relates to how companies allocate resources to high-value versus low-value areas.

In the picture above, we see the existence of a limber tail. The plunge can be attributed to clusters of freeloader products or loss-making customers. The products have high revenue and thin or negative margins and drag operating profits down. They are usually positioned in the eighty or ninety zones in the revenue matrix, but clearly, located on the right side of quadrant four in the contribution margin matrix. In other words, the plunge happens when companies sell large amounts of products with low or negative margins. The presence of a limber tail is a clear sign that the business should reevaluate its long tail strategy before adding more variants.

The plunge can also indicate that a company has run out of options, in the form of good margin customers or products. The demand for its long tail items is limited, and the business is consuming too much overhead to handle the low-volume SKUs. It implies that the firm is compromising its bottom line by selling at or below its complexity costs. Unfortunately, in most cases, companies don't have a plan to eliminate the plunge, or even worse, do not have a reasonable strategy to support this exception. A typical example is when prices remain flat or decrease over the years on high-volume products, without the corresponding cost or price improvements. A gradual margin erosion occurs, but the customers buying at a loss continue to be deemed "strategic" by managers.

Virtual marketplaces such as Amazon and Alibaba, with nearly unlimited shelf-space and low-cost access to global markets, do not usually see a plunge in true profitability. Their true profitability curves are closer to the contribution margin curves with a more gradual slope, compared to manufacturing businesses, for example. The cost of adding new products to the tail is low and well defined. Instead of making products in-house, they've created a way to add products to the long tail using virtually zero overhead. This supply chain model, known as a virtual marketplace, means that suppliers carry the cost of sourcing and handling the low volume. Still, virtual resellers can run into freeloaders or CRaP, as defined by Amazon, if the item is stocked at their warehouses and has costly logistical requirements (bulky and heavy, for example). However, there are only a few freeloaders compared to millions of moneymaking items in Amazon's long tail, for example.

Acquiring valuable insight, quad by quad

Quad one is the business core and the head of the demand curve. Any improvement to Q1 will have a disproportionally positive impact on true profitability. The central management challenge if to make this area more substantial and more profitable, treating this quad as if it were a stand-alone business. Managers must learn all they can learn about core customers and products - margin issues (price, variable cost), market segments, distribution channels, competitive threats, and much more. What would we do differently if this was a stand-alone business?

We want to make the head of the demand curve as big and as lucrative as we can since this is where true profitability rises fast, at the head of the curve. No matter what we do to the tail, we can't fix the endpoint if we have a profit margin deficit in Q1. Companies must strive to be the lowest-cost producer or retailer at the core. The best supply chain, with the most economical material cost, will always be the winner. If you are a manufacturer, you will want to delve into the bill of materials for each product, using value engineering and value analysis to optimize specifications and reduce material cost.

A deadly mistake is trying to build a business by making the tail long enough, in any product category, without first strengthening the core. It's the proverbial "tail wagging the dog." The internet is full of stories about well-intentioned product curators that failed early on, like Ecomom, Boo.com, Pets.com, and many more. Part of the reason why so many online startups fail is that they ignore the cost of complexity when growing via sourcing and selling low volumes of hard-to-find items to too many customers. Logistical costs, customer support intensity, returns and recalls, advertising expenses and supply chain disruptions are some of the factors that eat up cash quickly and break the company when there is no business core to hold on.

These e-tailers failed because they got lost in the complexity and were never able to charge for it. Perhaps, they never bothered to find out the differences between Q1 and Q4 or head and tail. No company can afford to build a very long tail without a profitable core. Although every company has a Q1, the proportions between high and low-value businesses are not always favorable. Moreover, applying the same supply chain and marketing models across the entire portfolio is also not a very good idea. Not all customers are equal, and you shouldn't provide the same level of support between Q1 and Q2 customers, for example.

The low-volume customers in Q2 should be attracted to your company because of your core products and services. At least that's the way it should be. Some come because of your value proposition and expertise in a given product or service category. Many come because of pricing and the vast selection of products. The mix of what Q2 clients buy should lean towards core SKUs, with minimal cost to serve. However, Q2 customers buy a blend of eighty and twenty products in reduced amounts, creating a massive number of transactions and collectively, needing much support, especially in the residual area or Q4.

Still, not even all supporting customers have the same value. There are both money-making and money-losing buyers, as well as large customers oscillating between the core and the transitional areas. There are also small and strategic clients, with potential to become eighty clients someday – the "baby whales." The data in Q2 is typically less dense, but it's suitable for recognizing demographical clusters, buying habits, and channels within the customer base. We use data to compare market segments via cluster analysis and to study transactional and purchasing patterns, such as mix. Savvy online retailers use analytics to decide how to invest direct marketing dollars. They mine for customers that buy a more favorable mix, spend more money, purchase more often, and yield better margins. These buyers receive additional attention and special offers from time to time.

As with product variety, having lots of supporting customers can be profitable if you have low transaction costs, charging for complexity in your margins.

However, companies with limber tails can lift profitability by merely cutting some level of residual customers at the end of the curve, especially low-volume and low-margin ones, with high transaction costs and minimal growth potential. Typically, these customers buy an unfavorable product mix, heavily weighted towards ancillary products in Q3.

Ancillary products sell to both core customers in Q1 and to noncore in Q4. Ideally, the bulk of the revenues from twenty products should be generated by eighty customers in Q3, but that is not often the case. Many businesses fill their offerings with dumb variety – or variants that have no purpose other than to appeal to twenty customers. Proliferation happens when we increase sales of low-volume, one-of-a-kind, or customized products to noncore clients. Custom products carry unique components and are expensive to produce, source, handle, and stock. They create detrimental complexity, which adds no value. A reduction in the number of ancillary SKUs is very useful in bringing down the number of discrete components, suppliers, inventory cost, and overhead.

Managers will add the dumb kind of variety when they try too hard to penetrate new markets and gain customers, expanding the product portfolio too quickly. The Dutch company Phillips, during the first decade of the millennium, is a case study for the detrimental effects of product proliferation[iv]. During those ten years, profits were mostly wiped out, and market capitalization fell significantly. Despite its performance, Phillips was the top patent filer in Europe and among the top 10 in the United States. It was active in more than 60 product categories by 2011. The company leaders in different business units and geographies were busy innovating and creating product variants for their markets and regions. However, the company failed to have an integrated view of its global product portfolio, to direct the innovation and variety towards the global eighty customers, instead of the global twenty. We can only imagine the size of Q4 for Phillip's during those days. The complexity almost destroyed the company.

Prolific innovation and agile product introduction can be fatal, if not focused on the high-value and potential areas of the business. To create a smart kind of variety, the type that attracts new customers, managers need an integrated view of their portfolios, using data to understand true profitability. From the product side, innovation should also help foster standardization and modularity. From the customer angle, we should focus on solving pain points and jobs to be done by our core and transitional clients. True profitability is an excellent way to guide product management on portfolio expansion decisions. Supporting products, to be developed and sold to low-volume customers, must clear a higher complexity cost hurdle. The only ways to avoid CRaP or freeloaders from eroding your bottom-line is to get paid for complexity or to filter-out products with low or no true profitability.

Without smart variety, companies quickly default to expanding the low-value and residual areas, represented by Q4 in the matrix. While this quadrant can be enormous in proportion to other quads, the data is lumpy and sparse, due to large numbers of small transactions and clusters of freeloaders. This quad is located almost entirely in the long tail and adds up to a fraction of the total revenue and margin. However, there is a lot of activity and complexity that goes on here. For masters of complexity, operating in this area is the same as offering a valuable service to customers, by which they make one-of-a-kind products and services available to many small buyers. At the limit, they serve a single customer buying one unit of a single product during the year. This service adds value to the company if it creates positive free cash flow and attracts new profitable customers.

The challenge with this quadrant is that it requires constant pruning and management attention to keep it from destroying value. It's not uncommon for companies to carry lots of high-volume / low-profit outliers for years, without bothering to reprice or to phase them out. General accounting and standard product management metrics are just not capable of dealing with these anomalies, resulting in limber tails and clusters of CRaP. For a long tail to be a good customer magnet, it must have minimum overhead under an unconventional supply chain model. There can be no emotional decisions when populating the long tail with goods to sell. The "not-invented-here" and the "not-made-here" paradigms should not apply. You want to create smart variety with smart sourcing.

Whenever manufacturers are adding SKUs to their long tails, if they are not leveraging existing eighty products or components, they should consider outsourcing their needs to vendors who possess domain expertise in such products. Outsourcing is a way to enhance the offering and to ensure that you always know the real cost (or most of it) based on what you pay your supplier for the item. Making Q4-only products in-house is still more expensive than buying them from the outside, even if you think you have an edge on variable cost.

Doing business in Q4 is equivalent to working in the chaos zone of the complexity model. The more business you do closer to the lower right corner of the matrix, the more difficult it is to figure out the contribution to the bottom line. General accounting will not tell you if you are making or losing money here. We call this the "madness zone." The further you move in the direction of the upper left corner, the simpler it gets. Operating in Q1 is more straightforward because you know your costs. At least you should! The more you know, the less you hesitate to make decisions. The rules of operation and the improvement strategies for these complexity zones are different. The graph below shows the complexity state for each area of the 80/20 matrix.

3.3 Portfolio complexity zones

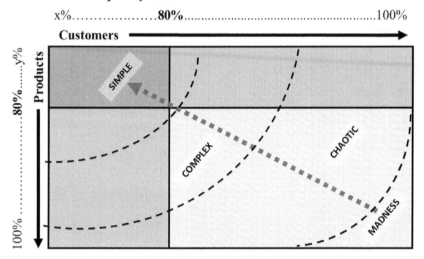

To become masters of complexity, companies need to learn how to maximize true profitability and attract new customers while staying away from chaos and madness. The more in-house value a business adds to its products or services, the easier it is to migrate towards the chaotic and madness zones of the matrix. High value-added products have better contribution margins, but they also attract a lot of overhead and complexity costs. Adding more value to products in Q1 is an excellent idea while adding more value to products in Q4 is a terrible one! Manufacturers can learn from long tail savvy retailers and adopt a hybrid, distribution-like model to profit from the tail-end, outsourcing more to suppliers, instead of tailoring and multiplying variants in-house. Even the large, online retailers, are always looking for new ways to outsource more, both at the core and at the tail. The growth in high-volume private labeled items is a way to offer a price-point SKU while challenging the existing supplier to become more competitive.

Whether they want it or not, companies will always have a long tail, and a certain amount of low-value business gathered in Q4. Nevertheless, managers have the option to make the long tail work for or against them. To make it profitable, they must continuously veer the portfolio towards the simple and complex zones, staying away from the madness area and reducing the exposure to chaos by controlling the tail size, slope, and anomalies. The tail size is controlled by deciding which products to introduce and how-to price, discontinue or fire money-losing SKUs and customers, using true profitability as a guide.

Managers can also achieve a less abrupt fall in true profitability by reducing the overhead associated with sourcing and selling in the long tail – adjusting the supply chain model, using virtual marketplaces and outsourcing more, for example. They eliminate anomalies by attacking clusters of freeloaders and addressing SKUs with low or negative true profitability. In the end, we need clear, data-based reasons to be doing much business in the chaotic and madness regions. If we don't shrink these areas, they will grow on their own and destroy profitability. 80/20 analytics is the best way to illuminate the portfolio, to make the long tail work for the business and not against it.

The logic behind True Profitability

We know that the many low-volume products that make up the twenty, in quads two, three, and four, are responsible for eighty percent of the total complexity cost. Q1 products and customers, on the other hand, are responsible for a much smaller portion of the overhead. The proportions are never so precise as 80/20, but there is always a discrepancy of such magnitude. We can quickly realize this imbalance by visualizing the same matrix under two different criteria. The one based on contribution margin (or revenue) will show a predominant Q1, versus the other quads. If we also draw the same model using complexity this time, we will realize that Q1 is relatively a lot smaller. Activity is a good proxy for complexity, in the form of customers plus products, transactions, or the part count, to cite a few.

To calculate true product profitability for any given product, we need to subtract the cost of complexity from the contribution margin. Most companies should have contribution or variable margin data by product, readily available from accounting systems. Regarding complexity cost, we must use the 80/20 matrix to determine the amount carried by each SKU, based on three factors: the total overhead in the business, the level of activity or transactions created by the specific SKU and its position in the matrix.

3.4 True Profitability Factors

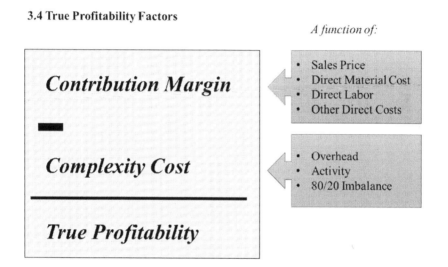

The overhead used in complexity cost is the total indirect cost below the variable margin line or everything that does not vary with production volume. It typically includes the fixed production expenses (in the gross margin) plus the ESG&A (engineering, selling, general and administrative) expenses, below the gross profit line. Companies that use Direct Cost accounting, instead of the traditional Absorption Cost, use a separate line in the P&L to track fixed production costs. They call these expenses period costs.

Direct costing is a specific form of cost analysis

that only uses variable costs to make decisions. It does not consider fixed costs, which are assumed to be associated with the periods in which they were incurred. In brief, direct costing is the analysis of incremental costs, for example, the expenses consumed when you manufacture a product; the additional increase in costs when you ramp up production; the costs that disappear when you shut down a production line; the costs that go away when you shut down an entire subsidiary. Unfortunately, fewer businesses use direct costing compared to absorption cost accounting. The ones that use direct costing, typically understand the value of managing complexity actively.

The way you decide to use fixed costs, i.e., in conjunction with ESG&A or separately, depends on the accuracy of the data. Most companies do distribute the fixed production costs to individual products to arrive at the gross profit, based on some allocation method. In our experience, we occasionally find a high correlation between the allocated fixed cost and revenue from each SKU. This link tells me that the allocation method used was not based on direct activity drivers, therefore not very useful. In such cases, we are better off combining period or fixed costs with ESG&A and distributing all expenses according to 80/20.

In general, companies base the allocation of fixed costs on direct activity indicators, such as labor or energy consumption during production. Many distributors use transaction volume or space consumed in the warehouse to assign fixed costs. We must first verify the allocation criteria and the integrity of the data, but, in such instances, we can use the fixed cost number assigned by accounting for each SKU and distribute the ESG&A based on 80/20 analytics.

To calculate complexity cost, we first position each SKU in the two-by-two matrix using contribution margin, as explained before. Second, we determine a complexity index or the number of complexity units that exist in each quadrant. Third, we distribute the total overhead in proportion to complexity units. Fourth we determine the amount of complexity cost carried by each SKU in each quadrant, in proportion to revenue, before calculating the individual true profitability. Below are the necessary steps to the complete sequence for each SKU.

3.5 Steps to arrive at True Profitability

SKU Value & Position
Determine the position in the two-by-two matrix and contribution margin

Complexity Units
Active cells, parts-count, transaction volume or a combination of factors

Complexity Cost by Quad
Distribute the overhead cost to the quads in proportion to Complexity Units

Complexity Cost by SKU
Distribute the complexity cost in the quad to each SKU in proportion to revenue

True Profitability by SKU
Contribution Margin minus Complexity Cost

80/20 analytics is not a financial or accounting system – it uses concepts and redeploys information from conventional methods to give you a different view of your portfolio. Complexity units measure the relative activity volume amongst the quadrants, but there is more than a single formula that can be applied. It depends on what mostly drives complexity in the business. For instance, if you are a manufacturer with lots of variants in Q3, trying to simplify your offering, you may want to use part count in each quadrant to calculate complexity units. Now, if you are a distributor, trying to reduce the cost to serve, you may want to use the number of transactions (invoices, calls, returns) in each quadrant. The most used and straightforward method is to add up all the active cells at the intersection of customers and products in the matrix. You can also use the sum of products and customers in each quad. These methods are not dissimilar to how ABC uses the activity as a proxy for complexity.

Alternatively, you may want to use a combination of factors to create a composite complexity index, such as active cells times revenue, or the number of people times transactions or the sum of individual parts in your sales mix, for example. Defining a generic index may sound subjective, but it can help as a KPI to track progress towards simplification. Remember that the index is not an absolute number, but a relative measure of complexity between the areas of the matrix. A simple to understand pointer that will give everyone a warning sign, to take a closer look at the data.

Beyond contribution and gross margins

To recognize the full impact of complexity and improve our ability to manage the portfolio, we must combine contribution margin (CM) with true profitability (TrP). CM gives us a ratio between price and direct cost; in other words, how the market values the company's cost-benefit equation. TrP is an internal metric and evaluates how productive or efficient is the company when creating and making products available.

A practical means to combine these two metrics, and yet another way to look at overall efficiency, is to track the ratio between contribution margin and overhead dollars associated with a product. Some companies call this KPI gross margin 2 or GM2 since it helps to compare two products for their ability to generate profits based on dollar returns over the invested cost or overhead. As an example, let's consider four products, which have equal contribution margin percentages, each placed at a different point in the profitability curve. The total overhead is the product's share of indirect or fixed manufacturing costs plus admin expenses (ESG&A), distributed according to the 80/20 method.

3.6 True Profitability and Gross Margin 2 (GM2)

	SKU "A" (Quad 1)	SKU "B" (Quad 2)	SKU "C" (Quad 3)	SKU "D" (Quad 4)
	Core	**Transitional**	**Supporting**	**Residual**
Revenue $	65,000	6,000	3,000	500
CM $	19,500	1,800	900	150
	30%	30%	30%	30%
Overhead $	(2,000)	(1,600)	(1,000)	(750)
TrP $	17,500	200	(100)	(750)
	27%	3%	(3%)	(150%)
GM2	9.8	1.1	0.9	0.2

Item "A" is a core product, in quadrant one, and generates high revenue at a 30% contribution margin. This SKU is the one with the highest dollar contribution and true profitability margin (27%). Despite the high income, it ends up with a smaller overhead apportionment relative to sales because quadrant one has fewer complexity units compared to other quadrants. The GM2 ratio for this SKU is very high, meaning that the profit it earns from customers is enough to cover 9.8 times the sum of expenses it consumes.

As a money-making bestseller, the company should protect and develop this item. Protecting means creating a moat around the product, learning everything we can about the competition, mitigating threats, and ensuring that it has the best supply chain and manufacturing resources. To develop is to look for ways to sell more of this product, or to sell more of its components, to customers in Q2, using dedicated sales account and support teams, for example. The high GM2 confirms that we have plenty of room to maneuver if we want to use pricing as a lever. It also says that the contribution margin can be used by the organization as a standard metric to evaluate sales and cost reduction performance.

Product "B" is a transitional product (80% to 90%) in quadrant two, and despite having the same contribution margin percentage as product "A" (30%) it receives a higher complexity cost allotment in proportion to sales, dropping its TrP margin to only 3%. We would need to dig deeper to understand why the low margin, but one possibility is an unfavorable sales mix towards low-volume customers. There could be excessive sales and support transactions involved in selling this SKU, and with a GM2 just above one, it can narrowly support its weight. The company should use TrP and GM2 to monitor the performance of this SKU, ensuring that it does not become a freeloader.

Although product "C" is also at a 30% CM, it's close to the break-even point; it shows a small loss at the TrP margin level (-3%). This SKU is a quadrant three item, and the first thing we need to understand is who are the customers for this product. Are most of the revenues created by eighty or by twenty customers? The answer to this question helps us decide whether we should fix the TrP margin issue right away or if we should look at this loss in the context of supporting valuable eighty customers. If this product is created primarily on the behest of a core customer and a more profitable one cannot replace it, the company might have to take the loss in the context of the total customer P&L, at least until they can find the time and resources to cut cost or renegotiate the price. However, if the primary buyers for this SKU are twenty or low-volume customers, the company can use pricing to close the TrP gap and avoid this item from becoming a freeloader.

The next item or "D" is a freeloader. This SKU is

at the tail of the demand curve in Q4, and it weighs down on the operating income since it doesn't generate enough CM to offset the high cost of complexity in this quadrant. It's currently not contributing to overall profitability. Only looking at contribution margin (30%) may lead us to believe that this is a profitable product when, in reality, "D" is more like a lost cause. The TrP and the GM2 are so low that you may need to replace or discontinue this SKU. By simply phasing-out such SKUs along with the associated overhead, the company will improve its bottom line.

Contribution margins or gross margins alone are not enough to manage a product portfolio, especially one with a long tail. The traditional accounting metrics are misleading when it comes to true profitability. Managers need to add the context and granularity offered by 80/20 analytics to understand the whole picture. The other deduction is that it is tough to make money in the lower-right corner of quadrant four, which coincides with the chaotic areas of the matrix. The best we can do is to shrink quadrant four instead of trying to fix the viability of large numbers of freeloaders. Managers don't have enough time in the day to do that, plus it would be wasted effort in the wrong direction. They should base their tail offerings only on products that have positive TrP or on outsourced SKUs, which is easier to determine the actual cost by looking at the vendor's invoice.

Managers can also use TrP and GM2 to measure

the performance of an entire product line, business unit, or company since the sum of all individual TrPs equals the total operating profit. They can also apply GM2 at a macro level to compare different portfolios and companies. For instance, manufacturing businesses with products delivering contribution margins in the upper 30's or lower 40's, and total overhead in the range of 15% of sales, tend to have GM2s between two and three. However, if the contribution margins are between 20% and 30%, the company will have to reduce overhead to about 10% of sales, to have a GM2 around two. Based on experience, manufacturing companies with a GM2 between two and three are the ones that can be called scalable. They can maintain higher profit margins during downturns. See ITW and Toyota as examples. These companies return far superior profit margins as they grow and stay between a GM2 of two and three. Companies that wait to fix GM2, only after it has dropped closer to one, are the ones that spend more effort and money to get back in shape during a downturn.

Conditioning of the long tail

Before a business can expand its long tail profitably and deliver increased variety to customers, it must first recondition its offering by acting on three fronts: getting rid of the freeloaders, turning the keepers into money-making items and developing a means to add and delete products with speed and confidence. Fixing the long tail is a team effort and requires data analysis and insights from 80/20 thinking to direct the work and track results.

The first and faster step is to challenge the loss-making products by cutting down and simplifying the portfolio, employing the SKU true profitability as a guide. We start by visualizing the path from peak margin dollars, at the head of the demand curve, to the final and total operating profit at the end of the long tail. It's a simple way to recognize contributors and detractors and to realize how we end up with the money we get to keep in our pockets. To build the curve, we start with a product table containing CM and TrP data, classified using the Pareto distribution. After we plot the profit amounts on Y and product variants on X, the endpoint of the curve should coincide with the total operating profit dollars shown in the company's P&L.

The following example and pictures depict a generic industrial manufacturer with sales of 250 million and operating profit of 4 million or 1.6% of revenue. The initial portfolio contained approximately 480 SKUs, with a very high degree of customization. The business had minimal net profits and was not generating enough cash. Here's how the profitability curve looked like when they started to tackle complexity.

3.7 Typical True Profitability Curve: Freeloaders and Limber Tail

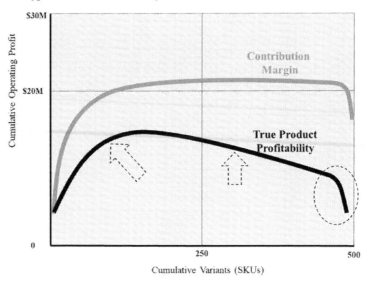

Cumulative Variants (SKUs)

In the chart above, we notice a sharp rise in true profitability, at the head of the curve, reaching the 14-million-dollar mark, only to start giving most of it back throughout the long tail. The result is an operating profit of just 4 million dollars! It means that 10 million dollars were taken away by complexity cost, in the form of overhead, freeloaders, and loss-making customers. The oval shape shows the limp tail, which is responsible for a significant portion of the damage. Several inflection points are likely to be caused by pockets of freeloaders. The left arrow indicates the behavior of core and transitional products and the position where profit starts declining. The company was funding the existence of its long tail with the free cash flow from eighty products.

If a business needs a very long tail to grow and sell

the most lucrative items at the head of the curve, it must have a large and profitable quad one to boost true profitability as high as possible. In our example, the larger the tail, the bigger and healthier the head needs to be to create a powerful wave that can overcome bumps along the way. The head is typically more profitable because the cost of complexity, in proportion to revenue, is less pronounced in quadrant one. Therefore, most of the contribution margin in this quad flow directly to the bottom line since it carries less overhead in proportion to sales. When companies know the direct and exact cost of eighty products, they can use contribution margin to help guide pricing decisions.

Almost every business knows which are the best-selling products or services that make them money. They also know the high-volume ones that are not so profitable. Therefore, companies tend to focus their optimization efforts on these high-stakes products or services which commonly fall in quadrant one. The smaller amounts of overhead allocated to core products is primarily a result of their physical separation from low-volume SKUs, which allows for better management, higher productivity, and direct cost accounting (fewer allocations). The production of these vital few high-volume products takes place on dedicated lines or in-lines, with more automation, faster throughput, and no setups. Overall there is a higher degree of focus and attention to core products by everyone.

To lift total operating profit, managers must protect and expand the core, fix the exceptions, and challenge the freeloaders at the end of the long tail. For the most part, they use pricing and forced attrition (products and customers) to get the job done. The pricing and simplification actions will inevitably shorten the length of the long tail, at least until they can fix the remaining SKUs and retake growth. We compare this phase to the pruning of a tree. By cutting its limb branches, and getting rid of problem areas, the tree can grow stronger again. The pruning addresses external complexity, for example, the types of issues that are caused by excessive customization and lack of similarity amongst the bills of materials sold. Companies should expect a small reduction in revenues accompanied by an increase in operating profit dollars. Here's a depiction of the smoothened curve after streamlining.

3.8 Streamlined True Profitability Curve: Less Freeloaders

We notice a decrease in the size of the offering by about 15% however, the final operating profit is now close to 10 million dollars, or 6 million more than when we began, or a 150% improvement. The gain is primarily a function of cutting the limp tail, pricing up freeloaders and changing commercial terms and conditions to noncore customers. The peak of the TrP curve is now above 15 million dollars, as opposed to 14 million when we started. So far, the actions taken mostly by product management, sales, and marketing have achieved to refine the portfolio using true profitability as a filter.

While simplifying the offering, our company began taking concurrent steps to fix internal complexity issues that were preventing the business from generating cash and breaking through the ROS (Return on Sales) ceiling. The complexity that is internal to the organization is one of the biggest impediments to success and is highly correlated to how companies design and source products or services. To reduce and control the issue, they needed to simplify bills of materials, supply chains, and processes, adopting standards that everyone could embrace. The company also changed its product design philosophy from custom design to design-for-simplicity. Standardization is equivalent to applying Lean principles to engineering, procurement, and manufacturing to minimize waste and complexity at the source.

One of the most effective simplification strategies

is to reduce part count in the bills of materials (BOM). The higher the number of discrete components in the BOM the higher is the number of vendors, purchasing people, engineers, inventory, and manufacturing complications. The business urgently needed to boost reuse and similarity among the components used in its finished products. To reduce part count, they first explored BOM similarity levels, using 80/20 analytics to correlate components with SKUs. They started using the BOM similarity index as a KPI to track standardization progress. They've also created an 80/20 matrix linking parts to suppliers, to understand high and low-values areas within the supply chain.

The result of standardization is a reduction in the overall part count, suppliers, and associated overhead. There is less duplication and parts are reused more frequently, as a result of increased BOM similarity levels. The supply chain was optimized at the core, leveraging the firm's purchasing power with strategic suppliers. Regarding quadrant three, the company adopted a more transactional mindset with suppliers, including pricing auctions for standard components. They've also started a program to outsource more of the low-volume parts and final products with vendors. The manufacturing of all eighty products moved to high-throughput in-lines with dedicated equipment, with a clear separation between the high and low-volume at the shop floor. In short, the core business received a high dose of focus and support with the allocation of prime resources during this work.

For manufactured goods, materials represent a substantial portion of the COGS. Therefore, to improve the contribution margin, we must optimize the material cost of targeted eighty products, using specific techniques and a knowledgeable team. Direct material optimization or DMO is a more comprehensive approach because it combines traditional value engineering and value analysis (VE/VA) with design-for-simplicity principles, clean sheet costing and benchmarking, engaging strategic suppliers in the redesign stage. In a matter of months, the company began to realize the benefits of product specification and supply chain optimization initiatives, which eventually led to the transformation shown in the following chart.

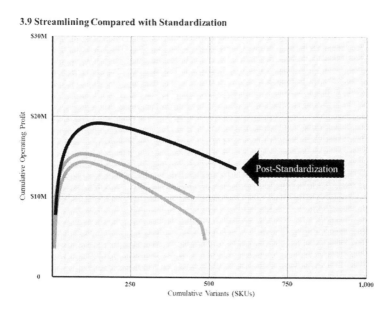

The after-standardization curve in the diagram above represents the impact of DMO on the company's P&L, which elevated the peak TrP from just above 15 million to 19 million. Decreases in material and complexity costs at the core will have a direct impact on the operating profit. The higher profitability of the eighty, combined with lowered overhead and higher outsourcing activity of twenty SKUs has lifted the total operating profit to approximately 14 million dollars. We notice an increase in the size of the portfolio, as the company starts adding back some variety using a better screening process and pricing mechanism based on true profitability.

To convert a company into a master of complexity, or one that uses large numbers of low-volume SKUs and variants to grow faster (long tail friendly), requires at least two fundamental changes to the business model. First, companies must enhance their product lines, moving towards modular architectures, from design-for-simplicity to design-for-variety. Modularity delivers ease of customization and upgrades without all the complexity and cost associated with nonstandard products. Second, businesses must govern complexity and actively manage their portfolios using data and true profitability, avoiding madness and chaos.

Modular designs benefit both customers and suppliers, offering greater customization flexibility, upgrade potential, manufacturing sustainability (reuse and remanufacturing) and lower support cost. It usually develops from the necessity to create large numbers of variants for different applications without resorting to nonstandard components. Modularity is a natural progression from standardization, and it's not an overnight exercise. It takes time to change the product architecture. However, we can realize its benefits even when we only apply modularity to future products. Almost always, the task of redesigning the entire portfolio for modularity is too costly and too daunting. Like standardization, companies will profit from modular designs even if they only apply it going forward, to new products and to product families that need to be optimized.

To keep standardization and modularity going while sustaining true profitability, companies need the discipline to govern complexity. We can't have a profitable long tail without actively controlling attrition, challenging money-losing SKUs, and customers. Variety and complexity have no use if they are not maximizing sales and profits. Our company, in the example, enhanced its product management and new product introduction processes with complexity leadership, 80/20 analytics, and true profitability. They use TrP to decide whether a product should enter or exit the portfolio, at what price and under what conditions. Good governance led to sustainable improvements in portfolio efficiency, reliable and innovative supply chain strategies. The picture below illustrates the outcome of modularization over time, compared to the other stages.

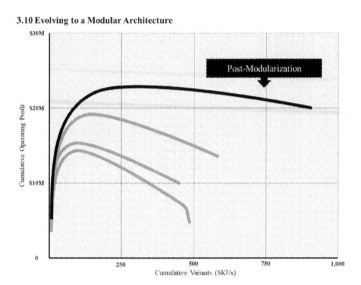

3.10 Evolving to a Modular Architecture

The after-modularization curve in the figure above shows a much enlarged and profitable core region, peaking at over 23 million dollars and well into the middle of the offering, which is a sign of a smaller residual area (quad four). We also see a flatter TrP curve, based on more outsourcing and less overhead required to carry low-volume products, while the offering has grown to almost twice the size as in the previous chart. The operating profit reached closer to 20 million or nearly five times the initial amount. The business turned into a robust free cash generator and was better prepared to expand the long tail and to endure market cycles.

This transformation took a couple of years to take place, but it's entirely achievable. The fact that we have a simple and objective, data-based analytical tool to track progress is an enormous advantage. In the following chapters, we will discuss the strategies and methods used to accomplish each of the phases above.

4 CHALLENGING FREELOADERS

When variety grows excessive, and proliferation takes hold, it's necessary to simplify the portfolio before expanding the long tail. Adding more items to a demand curve that has already too many inflection points and low-margin freeloaders will worsen the problem. The new variants will bring significantly more cost and cloud the data, making it harder to know if you are helping or hurting profits. To use another analogy, we must first clean the house before attempting to rearrange the furniture. 80/20 analytics is equivalent to sunlight. By illuminating the area with data, we put the focus on spots that need cleaning.

By streamlining the portfolio, we mean to increase true profitability with fewer SKUs by questioning loss-making products and customers. We start by determining the good and the not-so-good areas of the business in an exact, quantitative way. Then we formulate strategies and take actions to make the good even better and to deemphasize the not-so-good. At this stage, we will change the way we market products and deal with customers, impacting pricing, sales effort and incentives, product availability, channels, and payment terms to have the desired results. The data gives us the necessary level of granularity to apply discrete pricing strategies, based on where the product falls in the demand curve. Traditional marketing usually fails to recognize the complexity and true profitability when making changes to the portfolio.

Pricing is an essential means to rebalance the delicate value-to-complexity equation. 80/20 analytics confers managers the resolve and authority to challenge and abate bad businesses from the portfolio, in a usual, everyday manner. Managers adjust pricing systematically in low-value areas to recover the overhead and to reposition freeloaders, letting the market decide how much it's willing to pay for variety and availability. Pricing in high-value areas is more strategic and punctual, based on data and marketing strategy. Using 80/20, managers can choose separate tactics for low and high-value regions, targeting the underperforming more aggressively while protecting the core. In other words, 80/20 analytics gives sales and marketing the ability to price more confidently, with higher intensity and precision.

To make this chapter more useful, we will resort to a few examples from the beverage industry to explain streamlining. This industry can use some help since it abuses variety to differentiate brands and expand revenues, catering to new consumer tastes and niches all the time. The number of flavors, sugar-free options, packages, and channels has exploded, creating enormous complexity and overhead. Just think about how complicated it is to make and ship products to so many different countries, with multiple languages and different standards of package labeling, for example.

The product varieties are equivalent to stock-keeping units (SKUs), and their sheer numbers add significant complexity to global giants like Coca-Cola and PepsiCo. As we've discussed, the cost to handle each SKU is interwoven and hidden in the business, in the form of indirect production costs and overhead in areas like sales, engineering, and administration. Companies rarely make these costs visible, nor they allocate them at the individual SKU level. New beverage categories are massive contributors to proliferation and complexity in this industry. Emerging segments such as coconut water, craft beers, boutique wines, and other alcoholic beverages are expanding fast. Coconut water alone grows nearly 30 percent every year while some distributors of spirits handle as many as 15,000 SKUs[v].

Depending on where the SKU falls in the contribution margin matrix, managers have four essential ways to deal with freeloaders: raise prices, lower costs, substitute for a profitable product or simply phase-out the product altogether. The strategy and the intensity will depend on the product value (current and future), based on its contribution potential. If a company sells large quantities of high-value (core) products to strategic distributors with unacceptable margins, for example, it may not be so trivial to increase margins right away. It may have to find ways to either reduce costs or locate money-making substitutes before it can raise prices again.

Fizzy drinks are the eighty products and thus extremely valuable for companies like Coca-Cola and PepsiCo. The demand for these beverages is falling in developed markets like the US and Europe, and there is little these companies can do, in terms of pricing, to revert the trend. To protect and grow the core business, they must find new customers and channels in available markets and simultaneously add more best-sellers to the head of the demand curve, like bottled water. The fact that global beverage companies already sell in most places around the world means that future eighty customers and SKUs are more likely to be sitting in quadrants two and three, waiting to be identified and developed.

On the other hand, there is more flexibility to deal with low-value SKUs as they can be more easily priced-up or phased-out. Nevertheless, the answer will always depend on the customer base nature, true profitability, and where the product falls in the demand curve. If a freeloader sells in quadrant three to a large distributor, the company may have to continue trading until it finds a more lucrative alternative. However, if a freeloader has sales in quadrant four, unless the product is essential to a high potential customer (baby whale), the company must adjust prices enough to have positive TrP. Pricing for complexity, using true profitability as a metric, is an effective way to challenge the reasons why we should keep selling freeloaders to low-value customers. Low-value products that sell primarily to small customers must have a higher margin threshold to compensate for complexity.

There are no fixed rules when choosing the actions for different areas of the matrix. Each case is unique. However, we can picture the various decision paths used by managers based on the alternatives discussed above and best practices. The decision trees below are two examples of the logic behind the choices, based on the product location in the matrix.

First, for core products, where price increases are not the first choice.

4.1.1 Decision Tree based on True Profitability for Core Products (The Eighty)

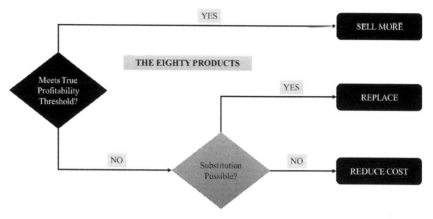

Second, for supporting products, where decisions are primarily influenced by the customer type (eighty or twenty).

4.1.2 Decision Tree based on True Profitability for Supporting Products (The Twenty)

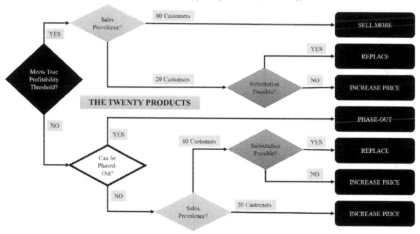

Along with the marketing strategy, the other critical decision drivers are the product position in the two-by-two model, contribution margin, and TrP. As we study each quadrant, it will be useful to have clear improvement objectives and margin goals for each one. To get to the improvement objectives, we ask three simple questions: 1) How can we make this quadrant better? 2) What is preventing us from making it better? 3) How will it look like when we get there? Then we pick the margin goals or thresholds.

How much margin do you need?

During the analysis, we realize that there are significant differences amongst the quadrants. As far as contribution margin dollars, Q1 is typically between 65% and 75% of the total. Q2 and Q3 usually are in the range of 7.5% and 15% each, while Q4 is between 5% and 10%. There are no set standards for these proportions, and they vary with the nature of the business, but significant discrepancies in symmetry can be revealing about the condition of the demand curve. The main point is that Q1 is substantially more significant than the other quads in value and much smaller in complexity cost. Q4 is the opposite of Q1 - low in value and plentiful in complexity. It follows the Pareto rule!

Manufacturing businesses tend to have matrices with large residual quadrants, while distribution ones tend to display huge numbers of supporting products. Companies with fewer core customers tend to have vast amounts of low-volume variants. The proportions and the data density of each quadrant can give valuable insights into the health of the portfolio. When it comes to customers, Q1 is strategic while Q2 is transactional. When it comes to products, Q1 is core while Q3 is ancillary.

Quadrant one is the make-or-break area of the matrix. It needs to be protected and enhanced. The margin target for quadrant one is a function of the total profitability goal for the company's operating profit target. If the operating profit target is 15%, for example, the TrP goal for Q1 should be close to 15%, if you want to have a chance to hit the company's mark. TrP margins are essential KPIs for core products. According to the Pareto rule, the amount of complexity existing in Q1 should be the smallest of all four quadrants. Thus, because of the low overhead, TrP margin should only be a few points lower than the contribution margin. Hence, if you have an item with low TrP in Q1, it will almost certainly reveal a problem with the variable margin. True profitability in Q1 is highly correlated to the product cost and to the company's ability to source materials and manufacture products competitively.

Quadrant four is where most of the long tail lives. It needs to be cleaned, resized and made profitable. We use contribution margin as the primary KPI for each product sold in Q4. However, we also look at the sum of TrP dollars for this quadrant, since companies need to recover the overall cost of complexity. This quad typically carries the highest overhead of all quadrants, and the goal for Q4 is to be at or above the break-even point, as far as total TrP is concerned. A reduction in the size of Q4 will have a substantial positive effect in decreasing indirect manufacturing cost and SG&A; granted management releases the resources associated with the shrinkage of Q4. Remember that, whenever the total TrP for Q4 is below zero, there is more money to be made by streamlining the offering than there is in selling more. If you want to have a very long tail, you will need to ensure positive overall TrP and good contribution margins at individual SKU levels.

Quadrant three is the area prone to SKU proliferation. It needs to be simplified and managed. Much of the complexity cost in this quadrant comes from the indirect production cost and the engineering and management expenses linked with designing, sourcing, and manufacturing. Products located in the transition area (eighty to ninety percent) should have TrP levels close to those in Q1. Although they carry more overhead than Q1, they are higher-volume and waver between Q1 and Q3 frequently. The SKUs at the bottom of the quadrant, which is also at the end of the long tail, need to have positive contribution margins and break-even at the aggregate TrP level, like quadrant four.

Quadrant two holds many small customers, which can create complexity due to the volume of transactions and unfavorable purchasing mix. As margin targets, we use a similar approach to Q3, i.e., positive TrP for transitional customers and positive contribution margin plus break even or more for total TrP. We also use the data to identify different segments and channels and detect high potential customers early on (baby whales) since we want to have different commercial policies for each of these categories. If you are a distributor, you may have more than one sales channel - retail and wholesale, for example - and it is advisable to create two or more separate matrices to study each channel individually. The following table summarizes the margin thresholds and KPIs for each quadrant:

4.2 Margin Thresholds by Quadrant

QUAD 1	(0% to 80%)	▶ True Profitability = Operating Profit Target
QUAD 2		
Transition	(80% to 90%)	▶ True Profitability = Operating Profit Target
Residual	(90% to 100%)	▶ CM: positive & Total True Profitability >= 0
QUAD 3		
Transition	(80% to 90%)	▶ True Profitability = Q1 or individual goals
Residual	(90% to 100%)	▶ CM: Positive & Total True Profitability >= 0
QUAD 4	(80% to 100%)	▶ CM: Positive & Total True Profitability >= 0

Once we have margin references to calibrate each quadrant, we start challenging products (and customers) that are below our profitability standards. However, we must do this with perspective and granularity to avoid making mistakes, by creating supplemental 80/20 matrices whenever necessary and performing quad analysis for by each relevant segment in the portfolio.

Start by improving the core business

Trying to increase margins in quadrant one solely with pricing is tough, considering the volume risk and the strategic nature of customer relationships. Still, economic and commercial conditions do change regularly and call for price corrections to adapt to radical fluctuations in material costs, for example. The nuance here is that whenever adjusting Q1, we must account for the customer's true profitability and the entire mix of products they buy. We can't just look at products in isolation when dealing with core customers. In general, for the products that fall squarely in quad one, pricing takes a backseat to cost optimization and profitable growth.

The most substantial margin improvement opportunities in Q1 come from an intense focus on sales and supply chain optimization. We want to maximize true profitability while becoming the lowest-cost provider. We also want to take better care of our core customers versus our competitors. To do all that, we need to separate the eighty from the twenty, physically, and learn everything we can about buyers and products. Start with the core customer P&L, accounting for the total purchasing mix in quads one and three. The true profitability target for each customer should equal the overall TrP goal for Q1. If the total TrP for an eighty customer is below the mark, the issue could be related to low-margin variants in Q3, demanded by the same customer.

Considering the buying power of a core customer, it is not surprising that they throw their weight around and demand new variants and changes to existing products. This behavior is widespread in the automotive parts industry, for example, where original equipment manufacturers (OEMs) are always requiring modifications to accommodate design changes, placing the burden of complexity squarely at the supplier. We call this practice customer-induced complexity. An excellent way to detect this issue is to compare the purchasing mix for two or more core customers in the same market or application. You might find multiple variants for the same use with only small design modifications. Depending on the level of similarity between the bills of materials for these small-volume variants, you may have more or less complexity cost.

We also need a P&L for core products. The amounts of revenue and margin coming from both eighty and twenty customers will give us new ideas to change marketing policies. We can create unique sales incentives and use different terms and conditions for these buyers. If we have thin margins on core products sold to twenty customers, for example, you can always increase prices in Q2 or charge more for services like freight. Multiple tactics can be used to transact in Q2, from providing sales incentives to charging freight premiums on purchase orders below a certain weight or volume.

A common practice in the beverage industry is to offer distributors bundles of products at incentivized values. They typically sell a package of eighty and twenty products combined, at a lower price than they would charge if the customer bought all of them separately. This method is widespread in the consumer world from cable TV companies to fast-food restaurants, to cite a few. While this is an effective way to sell more eighty SKUs and influence the purchasing mix, it's not the only way to improve the size and profitability of the core business. Ensuring we are the lowest cost producer or retailer for eighty products is the best way to keep the core growing profitably in the long haul.

To be the lowest cost, we need the best supply or value chain. A useful exercise consists of grouping eighty products according to value streams, which represent sequences of activities required to design, source, produce, sell, and distribute a specific good or service. Value streams impact true profitability in different ways, such as procuring materials from low-cost-country vendors, manufacturing in highly efficient automated lines, employing dedicated sales account teams and using rapid delivery systems, and so on. For instance, companies often build a portion of their core products in less efficient production lines, which carry more overhead in the form of extra labor and setups. Separating the eight from the twenty and assigning the best value streams to the eighty are essential steps to improving the core. Eighty products need value chains that yield low-cost, high quality, fast delivery, and, as a general rule, should be manufactured in-house. Noncore businesses need cost-certainty and can be made in-house or outsourced to specialized suppliers. Outsourcing makes it simpler to place a value for these items since the cost is always known, based on the supplier's invoice.

Coca-Cola is fighting hard to avoid further erosion of its core products - fizzy drinks - while trying to grow sales of new beverages to replace lost revenue and profitability in quadrant one. Variety is one of the strategies used to attract new customers. The company carries 500 brands with more than 3,500 types of beverage in dozens of package sizes and configurations - up from 400 brands and 2,600 varieties in 2008. Sales of juices, flavored waters and teas are going up while sales and profitability of fizzy drinks continue to slide. The company has realized that fighting a price war for fizzy is not the right approach since the demand is falling due to changes in consumer taste. The plan used by the company to protect the core is to improve the value stream for its eighty products and reduce SKU proliferation of fizzy while adding useful variety at the tail.

Coke owns the bottling operations in North America, which have suffered from low performance in recent years. Also, throughout its roughly 130-year existence, the company offered an increasing variety of can sizes and bottles for its eighty products, while the average volume per container grew significantly. As a result of SKU proliferation and evolving consumption patterns, many of the core products dropped to quadrant three. To protect the core business, Coke had to simultaneously improve manufacturing and distribution value streams in North America, simplify the portfolio of eighty SKUs and add variety to its long tail to attract new consumers. The offering simplification caused a reduction in the number of SKUs, consolidating the eighty products into fewer bottles and can sizes, including 6.5 and 8 oz cans. While consumption changes will continue to impact the sales mix at the core, sales of these new SKUs are growing 10 to 15 percent annually[vi].

Coke's example illustrates the value of SKU simplification and the importance of managing complexity and variety to attract new customers. It also shows an in-depth knowledge of the consumption patterns and the power of data-driven strategies. Once you have a better understanding of your core business, you can turn your attention to the end of the demand curve to deal with the limber tail.

Fix the drop at the end of the long tail

A steep decline in true profitability at the end of the long tail means that a cluster of high-volume, money-losing products (or customers), is still active in the portfolio. By merely cutting or fixing the tail end, we can add back a significant amount of money to the operating profit. There can be different causes for the limber tail, such as systemic material cost challenges affecting an entire product line, for example. Another common reason is often the existence of large loss-making customers.

Companies can keep losing money for a long time with "strategic customers," as deemed by management. In most cases, there is no clear plan or path to fixing the issues that created the problem. Instead of baby whales, organizations create "sharks" by throwing away profits via poorly negotiated contracts and price reductions under the guise of customer-demanded productivity. Material economics, low-cost country sourcing, and currency fluctuations are some of the reasons used to justify price reductions over time. The fact is that price cuts must be accompanied by immediate and equal cost reductions to sustain margins. If the business fails to lower direct costs, in sync with price decreases given to high-volume customers, the margin gap will increase rapidly.

Loss-making customers usually buy large quantities of freeloaders. In the revenue matrix, they are located either in quads one or two; however, when we switch to contribution margins, they quickly fall back to the end of Q2. In general, they have unique and unprofitable purchasing mixes and buy too many freeloaders in large quantities. Not many profitable shoppers order the same SKUs that these customers buy, at least not in high amounts. In Amazon's parlance, they buy too much CRaP.

The approach used in business-to-business is to renegotiate the rules of the trade with these customers. They should know that you are losing money with their business and that your company would be better off without them. It would be nice if we could identify substitutes for all the freeloader items they buy, before having these discussions, but rarely one can replace the entire offering. Realistically, managers will have to negotiate significant price increases and mix changes to recover margins or stop selling the freeloaders, which can sometimes lead to ending the relationship with the customer.

Managers should be prepared to divest some low-value buyers and stop selling products or services at a loss if they can't fix the issues. Customer divestiture is a viable option since it releases resources from a residual operation to core areas of the business. Retaining an unprofitable low-value customer at all costs, for a long time, is not a sustainable strategic choice. Data and sound judgment are essential to avoid mistakes when deciding to part ways. In my experience, however, we've seen more customers accepting price increases than walking away. Service levels, quality, and reliability are plausible reasons why customers stick around, aside from low cost. Changing supply sources or having to re-engineer a new component into their products might also be deterrents. In the end, managers should not shy away from pursuing pricing corrections to fix the issue. Both scenarios, i.e., pay the new price or leave, contribute to raising the company's operating profit in this situation.

Sometimes the business is just swimming in the red ocean. It's trying hard to enter uncompetitive segments or geographies, i.e., markets that are not profitable for its business model or the products or services it sells. Companies create clusters of freeloaders to enter unchartered territory and keep these money-losers going for too long. For instance, many firms attempt to penetrate emerging markets such as China and India without making the necessary modifications to their offering. The lack of pricing options and differences in performance expectations versus the local competition are some of the reasons why they fail to grow in these markets.

The Chinese beverage market is enormous but challenging to enter at the same time. Danish brewer Carlsberg arrived in China in 1981 and struggled for many years due to state-owned competition and the fact that Chinese consumers were accustomed to low-priced beer. Carlsberg was literary drowning in a red ocean made of beer. The situation went from bad to worse when the small breweries were rolled-up into state-owned giants like Tsingtao Brewery, Beijing Yanjing Brewery, and China Resources Snow Breweries. The beer market in China became highly unprofitable for foreign companies in the nineties. In 1999, Carlsberg effectively left China by selling its brewery and dismissing its employees. Recently Carlsberg returned to China under a different strategy, to play only in profitable niches, and became successful in specific provinces in Western China[vii].

However, it's not just emerging countries that can present challenges. Companies get into trouble when they embark on revenue growth in mature, saturated, and developed regions as well. Trying to gain share in established markets or growing on too many fronts simultaneously, can create enormous transactional complexity and increase overhead faster than revenues and profits. One can evaluate the level of success when entering a new market by using the concept of portfolio momentum. Portfolio momentum is the organic growth a company achieves through the market growth of the segments represented in the portfolio. It measures how well the company is aligned with and performing within the market segment(s) it has selected to compete.

In its study of 416 US companies over two economic cycles, the authors of The Granularity of Growth found that portfolio momentum explains 46% of the difference in growth performance between large companies. Only 21 percent came from real market share gain, and 33% came from M&A (mergers & acquisitions). Portfolio momentum is known as the most effective form of organic growth there is when you can align your eighty products and services with the market[viii].

To measure the company's performance in each targeted segment, managers can use cluster analysis. By breaking the 80/20 data by target market or region, and performing quad analysis, we can learn how effectively these sectors are performing. The proportions and the data review will yield valuable insights - how large is the core business versus the low-value area, how profitable, how dense, and so on. Furthermore, if you have granular market data from outside research organizations, you can superpose the market eighty on top of your eighty to see how much momentum there is.

As an example, a construction and industrial equipment manufacturer uses 80/20 analytics to measure the performance of their dealers. They look at five different segments in the dealer data and compare those with the market figures published by external research organizations. The analysis shows how aligned is the dealer with the market activity, in terms of sales and inventory. It allows the dealer to change inventory dollars from supporting to core products continually, so they have immediate availability of the items at the head of the curve. It also allows for increased sales focus on the high-value segments of the market, which are continually changing. Without inventory analytics, they run the risk of prioritizing low-value products versus high-value ones.

Some familiar occupants of the tail end are product survivors or SKUs that should have been discontinued a long time ago. Typically, these are outliers launched with little or no margin and expected to make a profit as volumes went up. Even though sales never increased as per the original plan, these items remained. For one reason or another, they managed to survive scrutiny and continued to drag down the operating profit. The company never paid too much attention to the production or sourcing of these items since sales were never enough to put them on the radar screen. High-volume survivors deserve another look under a TrP filter, including a realistic reassessment of the demand forecast. Low-volume survivors need to be priced up or discontinued.

In summary, to lift operating profits, you must be prepared to prune the limber tail. You do that by renegotiating contracts, raising prices, replacing products, divesting customers, and abandoning unprofitable market segments and regions. We know that managers need both fact-based evidence and determination to implement stringent measures. 80/20 analytics is the essential means to justify management's position when making tough calls in the chaotic zone of the matrix, where there is less consensus on execution.

Cut the amount of low-value business in Q4

Most freeloaders and profit laggards, located at the end of the demand curve, reside in quad four. Therefore, to have a productive long tail, the offering must primarily contain low-volume products that exhibit true profitability — typically those that sell to both core and supporting customers alike. Having a long tail doesn't mean having a sizeable residual area. Sellers can offer a wide variety of small-volume items if they limit the size of Q4. The tail area should be dense with things that are simple to source and have low cost-to-serve. For instance, products that the company already makes and sells to core customers, as well as new items conceived to attract new prospects under a marketplace-like model.

While we will never be able to eliminate quad four, we must reduce its size and keep it small. Having most low-volume revenues coming from the residual area is a bad idea. Businesses can make more money by shrinking Q4 and eliminating the associated overhead than by selling more in that area. Maintaining this area small requires an active screening process to prevent sales, marketing, and engineering from launching new freeloaders without proper scrutiny. We will discuss the governing process in more detail in a later chapter.

Pricing is also critical to reduce and control the size of residual business. Managers should exercise pricing without fearing competition or sales losses in Q4. It's a waste of effort to try to fix each item in isolation for this quad. Remember that, while Q4 amounts to only five to ten percent of sales, it carries most of the complexity cost. The ability to minimize the amount of low-value activity is just as critical as having pricing power over high-value items. Still, there will be instances when pricing alone is not enough, and the company will need to eliminate SKUs. For example, those items that are beyond the point of recovery (hopeless) or survivors that continue losing money despite several corrections. The analytics will help single out freeloaders and loss-making customers with sales and purchases (80% or more) tied to Q4. These should be the primary targets for general price increases and other changes to reduce cost-to-serve.

The overall pricing increases applied to Q4 should be based on the TrP break-even target or the total amount of dollars required to reverse a loss in true profitability. Companies can use a uniform increase across-the-board or apply different pricing tiers based on channels, regions, or considering products and customers that fall in the transition area. Regardless of how we chose to do it, the pricing will have a positive impact - one way or the other. SKUs need to meet a higher threshold to cover the excessive overhead and expand the long tail profitably.

Boston Beer Company is known as the "largest microbrewery in the world." The company, founded in 1984, has reached $900 million in annual sales at an exceptional 51% gross margin (2014 annual report), distributing products all over the US plus 30 countries. The leading brand is Sam Adams, with more than 60 beer flavors, offering multiple varieties of malt beverages and hard cider under different names. Sam Adams' products are considered premium by the market and are at the core of the company's portfolio. Despite the massive scale and the fact that craft beer has much competition from local breweries, the company has always played well in the craft beer segment, with many innovations in terms of unique varieties of flavor and seasonal offerings.

Boston Beer Company is a successful example of how to align the business models with the different sectors of the demand curve. The company has effectively separated production, sales force, and distribution between eighty and twenty products. By focusing on core business, it delivers the lowest product cost to distributors of Sam Adams, without compromising quality. At the same time, it never stops experimenting with new beverage brands and flavors, behaving similarly to a microbrewery. While other companies act in similar ways, the difference is in the approach used to manage prices and the lifecycle of the twenty SKUs. The sales force of more than 400 employees is continually listening to customers and providing timely data to product management, allowing for quick decisions regarding the tail offering. The pricing agility and the ability to quickly phase new twenty products in and out gives Boston Beer Company an edge in this challenging beer market[ix].

Reduce SKU proliferation

Most of the customer-induced proliferation shows up in quadrant three. Although the data in Q3 reflects only sales to core customers, the product offering is a mix of medium and low-volume SKUs purchased by core and supporting customers. Complexity increases when we have large numbers of unique products sold to individual customers. For instance, large numbers of low-volume variants created for a single core customer or many unique products with irregular sales to low-volume customers. The density of the data in Q3 reveals how much business the company does on the behest of eighty customers versus twenty. This quad carries a lot of complexity cost associated with design, sourcing, manufacturing, and support. While pricing and sound product management will have a positive impact, lasting improvement comes from dealing with internal complexity issues and healing the product line.

Proliferation is also related to the product line architecture, reflecting upon the level of similarity amongst the bills of materials (BOM). Low levels of similarity drive more components and suppliers, thus adding cost. To heal the product line means to increase the ability to satisfy customer needs with fewer SKUs in the offering. By having a modular architecture, for example, companies can offer buyers more choices without increasing the number of different subcomponents in the BOM - the LEGO approach. However, to attain a modular architecture, first, we need to standardize the product line, by developing guidelines that help maximize compatibility and interoperability. Product line standardization boosts the reuse level for parts and components, thus optimizing the supply chain and reducing engineering and production costs.

As far as external complexity goes, the most significant opportunity in this area is to control the level of proliferation induced by eighty customers and improve the overall margin and true profitability. The goal is to simplify the offering, reducing cost and ensuring that each core customer is profitable. The data can show you the purchasing mix for every core customer, uncovering the revenue imbalance between eighty and twenty products. Buying more supporting products is less of an issue if the mix favors popular low-volume products at good margins. However, if a core customer buys significant quantities of unique, low-volume products, you are likely to have more cost and dedicated resources, in the form of specialized tooling, production lines, different parts, and suppliers.

You can also determine how much complexity cost each eighty customer drives by subtracting the contribution margin from TrP, in the customer P&L. The purchasing mix and the complexity cost compared to other customers are essential pieces of information when negotiating economics with a core customer. In the case of complexity-inducing clients, managers should attempt to simplify the tail, or the bottom part of Q3, instead of purely increasing prices in Q1. A reduction in the number of items is an excellent way to cut cost, and it can be measured objectively using 80/20 analytics. It's also common to incentivize eighty customers to reduce the number of variants and options, by sharing the savings from cost reductions. In my experience, core customers rarely understand the magnitude of the issue they create on suppliers. Managers should engage them by using comparative figures that show activity levels, such as the number of changes requested in a period, unique variants, and lack of similarity in the bill of materials.

Managers can use 80/20 analytics to single out products with most of their revenues tied to Q3 (80% or more) to learn about their distribution and concentration patterns: i.e., sold to one or few customers versus sold to many across the board. The revenue distribution across the customer base will help determine the simplification strategy. For example, we can look at similar products in Q3 (same application), with sales to multiple eighty customers, and evaluate the level of similarity in their BOMs. A good target for Q3 is to raise the similarity index for SKUs associated with families of products or applications.

At this stage, you want to understand the sources of variation, highlight potential simplification targets and start thinking about possible strategies to simplify the offering, such as redesigning two or more products to fit the same application, consolidating and reducing the number of discrete SKUs and so on. You will want to raise prices on the low-volume and low-value items, or the ones primarily sold to supporting customers in Q4. You may also want to consider carrying a little inventory and outsourcing the production of the low volume to new or existing suppliers. Other typical areas that are prone to simplification are:

- Low-volume products that are sold exclusively to supporting customers.
- Products and parts without sales for several years.
- Private-label SKUs with different part number or packaging.
- Similar items with varying quantities in each package.
- Different products for the same application, for different customers and markets.

- Low-volume products with unique (costly) production processes.
- Low-volume products out of your area of expertise – consider outsourcing.

Lastly, companies need product management or new product introduction teams to prevent the unprofitable business from entering Q3, including clear policies on customization and modification. They also need a clear position on tailored products: Who should get them and how they are to be priced and produced? Complexity governance will be the subject of a separate chapter in this book.

"Not all customers are created equal."

All customers are appreciated, but not all customers are profitable from a TrP perspective. The purchasing mix is the primary reason why some customers are profitable, and others are not. Customer TrP helps identify the ones which cost more to serve than they generate in contribution margin. Once the company recognizes the money losers, it can devise strategies to change them into profitable buyers or divest from these customers altogether.

The two primary goals for Q2 are to improve the

overall profitability and to convince twenty customers to buy more eighty products. Inducing purchasing mix changes to fix TrP, especially for those loss-making customers located in the transitional area, is a widely used approach. Other strategies range from segmentation to divestment. 80/20 analytics is essential to guide decisions related to mix, segmentation, and customer divestment.

Before we start making changes, we need to remember that there are at least two types of customers in Q2 which need to be singled out from all others – transitional zone ones and baby whales. Transitional customers, like the core ones, need to be individually profitable from a true profitability standpoint; therefore, we need to influence and turn their purchasing mix to become more favorable. Baby whales or supporting customers with high growth potential need individualized strategies to grow and become core someday. The remaining supporting customers should represent a variety of segments, regions, and channels. Managers need to decide if there are representative subgroups amongst them, which need to be studied separately.

If the analytics points to significant and discernible segments or niches, we can use 80/20 cluster analysis to compare the data sets, creating a two-by-two matrix for each grouping and correlating them with the main one. A twenty customer in the overall dataset can be an eighty customer in a market niche that you want to develop.

You can also use cluster analysis to make decisions about re-channeling small customers under other large ones, for example. Rather than shipping to multiple sites, consider finding a master distributor and channel the purchases from low-volume twenty buyers in the region to the wholesaler.

While you use the diversity of products to attract new buyers, you can use incentives and rebates to entice supporting customers to purchase more products from the head of the demand curve. Consequently, a key indicator is the overall sales mix of eighty versus twenty products in Q2. You also want to highlight customers that purchase more in Q4 than they do in Q2, as well as the ones below your contribution margin target.

Companies are continuously offering incentives and rebates to drive twenty customers to buy more high-value products and to improve their purchasing mix. There are multiples tactics, and there is a lot written about them but, in general, they fall into three categories: a) Increase per-customer sales with cross-selling and upselling; b) Retain customers by rewarding them and improving the customer experience and c) Lowering the cost to serve by moving some of the clients to lower-cost channels, as discussed above. One crucial aspect, however, is to always separate strategies, commercial terms, and service levels between the eighty and twenty, including sales and customer support. The top strategies used to streamline the supporting customer quadrant are:

- Differentiate service levels for supporting customers: require minimum order quantities, longer lead-times, special shipping charges based on lot sizes and different payment terms.
- Consider raising prices for clusters of supporting products primarily sold to Q2 customers. Do not hesitate to change pricing and commercial policies on core products marketed to Q2 customers at low or no margins.
- Develop incentives to bundle with or buy more core products to improve the purchasing mix. Use analytics to devise innovative cross-selling strategies.
- Re-channel and re-direct erratic, very low-volume customers to only buy other customers or distributors. Some low-volume customers will be better off buying from wholesalers.
- Discontinue persistent loss-making residual customers at the end of the curve. Exceptionally low-volume or low-margin, outside of the geographical area or distribution channel, with high transaction costs, with no or minimal growth potential and buying an unfavorable mix of products, for example.

While the above strategies are frequently used to streamline the portfolio, they do not exhaust all the possible scenarios we can come up with when using 80/20 analytics. The picture below helps bring these marketing-related and portfolio rationalization ideas together for each quadrant of the 80/20 matrix.

4.3 Rationalization Strategies by Quadrant

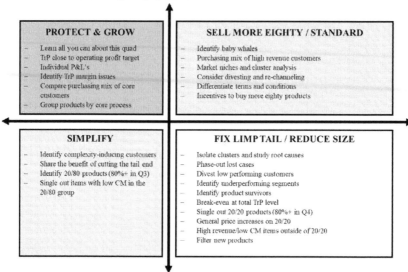

After cleaning up the product and customer portfolio with pricing and simplification strategies, we change our attention to attacking internal complexity to lift the profitability of the items that must remain in the offering. While we still have external opportunities, we must put our own house in order and reduce the chaos created by excessive part numbers, too many suppliers, lack of design standards, and sub-optimal manufacturing.

5 HEALING THE PORTFOLIO

More than 75% of all companies believe they have too much complexity, as they wrestle with excessive variety and proliferation. As products age, companies see swelling numbers of SKU variants tied to less profitable revenues. Large amounts of freeloaders reverberate throughout the business, increasing the overhead and limiting value creation and profitability. While growth is essential, the offering expansion in terms of the SKU numbers puts a heavy burden on the organization. The problem is not the expansion, but the extra complexity. Expanding the portfolio, without additional complexity, will always give higher margins.

Proliferation causes internal complexity, which is an inherent predicament when firms expand the business. Most times, it's self-inflicted while responding to competitive pressures, answering to immediate customer demands, entering new markets, or developing new products. Empirically, for more than 70% of manufacturers, SKU variety more than doubles over the lifecycle of a single product. Although external factors also contribute to internal complexity, such as integration efforts from mergers, acquisitions, and increased regulations, portfolio expansion is still the critical driver of internal complexity.

We can think of a business as an hourglass, where sand is equivalent to cash. One side represents profits, and the opposite chamber is overhead. You start with the profit side up, generating money from new markets and SKUs. As time goes by, cash flows to the bottom in the form of too many parts, high inventories, many production lines, unfocused processes, and excessive people. You must flip the hourglass upside down to regain balance and drain complexity cost. However, to always maintain a minimum level of resources on the cost side and have customers and products to sell, you must keep turning the hourglass from time to time. Think of the top end as external complexity. With time, gains give way to costs and, unless managers flip the hourglass, they will get stuck with too much internal complexity.

5.1 Internal and External Complexity

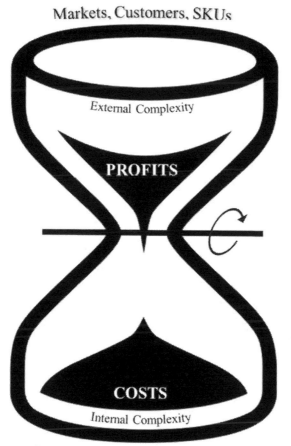

Markets, Customers, SKUs

External Complexity

PROFITS

COSTS

Internal Complexity

Parts, Suppliers, Inventories, ...

Governing complexity is equivalent to continuously finding the right balance between internal and external variety and diversification. It's never letting one side overpower the other - an exercise in dynamic equilibrium, and it can't be left alone. We've previously discussed how to rationalize the offering by challenging loss-making products and customers, to recover profits. Streamlining relies a great deal on pricing and product management actions. In this chapter, we will focus on how to reduce the complexity that is created inside the company, preparing the business to enlarge the long tail profitably. Standardization builds on the streamlined portfolio and uses product reengineering and supply chain strategies primarily to improve true profitability. Later, we will discuss how to maintain simplicity and govern the long tail while operating in the complexity zone.

How much internal complexity do you have?

A business can measure product line complexity in both direct and indirect ways. Direct metrics come from portfolio analytics, showing how products and components fit together to meet the range of external applications, in line with the product roadmap and strategy. One indicator, in this case, is the level of reuse and switchability of components within the bills of materials (BOMs) that form the offering. We call this KPI the BOM similarity index or SI for short.

A low or degrading similarity index is a strong indication that costs are going up due to the component's proliferation. For instance, if a manufacturer has a very long tail, it needs to have a higher SI for products sold in quadrant three, to have a positive overall true profitability. A high SI points to superior levels of reuse and switchability in the BOM, which is conducive to efficient supply chains and lower material costs. Elevated BOM similarity is also an indication of superior, modular product architecture. While there are no absolute standards for SI levels since product lines are unique, there are notable examples in each industry to use as benchmarks. Still, the positive evolution of this KPI is a relevant indicator of progress towards simplification.

Another indication of complexity is how similar products fulfill end-user needs in a specific market or application. Most companies offer tailoring or customization to a base product design, in the form of options or accessories. Recognizing that each small change in the BOM is a new SKU, it's useful to know the number of SKUs offered in similar markets or applications for each product family. It's normal to find numerous subtle variations in similar designs resulting in high numbers of SKUs developed for the same end-use and sold to different customers.

The question is not whether a company should customize or not but for which customers and under what conditions should the business tailor its products. A high number of custom specifications within a product family can be good or bad, depending on their true profitability (position in the matrix), sourcing and production processes used, as well as the product line architecture. A high number of tailored products in Q1 can mean something very different compared to elevated amounts in Q3, for example. Having 50% of the SKUs sold in Q1 based on the same core design, manufactured and sourced similarly, can be extremely profitable. However, a high number of custom specs in Q3 can be a problem, depending on the manufacturing and sourcing strategies used.

The more a company can leverage its high-efficiency, high-throughput production lines, and its high-volume supply chains to provide both core and supporting products, the better it gets. Manufacturers can always tweak or add accessories to an eighty SKU after they assemble the base product in high-throughput lines. However, the cost of adding a modification to a twenty product is typically much higher. Tracking SKU proliferation for different product families and customer groupings helps develop better manufacturing strategies and product line architectures.

Cummins (CMI) is a world leader in diesel engines and power generation. Its product line architecture is one that allows for high levels of reuse and switchability. Cummins develops engines in families or base configurations with a high degree of component similarity (SI) among the families. Then they offer various accessory bundles or options on top of the base engines that cater to several applications such as on-highway trucks, marine, and generator sets. Customers can also specify accessories that can either be mounted on engines or shipped together as a kit.

The advantage of this architecture is that it drives simplicity throughout the entire system, from sales to manufacturing. The company has taught everyone, including customers, how to use a standard engine specification language, based on the product architecture. The final price is related to the customization level within a market or application. The value of the business and the volumes determine the manufacturing strategy. Cummins uses bounded rationality to offer variety while controlling the levels of customization and proliferation.

A shocking realization is that most companies do not measure direct indicators of product line complexity. If you ask around for BOM and application similarity KPIs you might get plenty of blank stares. Only companies that value standardization and modularity, such as Toyota and Scania, use such metrics. For the most part, managers have some idea that complexity is hurting the business via indirect KPIs, but they cannot put their finger on the root causes right away. Managers feel the pain in areas like delivery performance, quality, indirect cost, supporting expenses, and return on capital.

Low SI impacts deliveries to customers since tailored parts interfere with standard products all the time, resulting in poor on-time and complete shipping performance. New components and engineering change modifications enter the system every day with little or no discussion. Furthermore, there is no process to eliminate unused or obsolete parts. As far as finished products or SKUs, there are significant numbers of products with minimal sales, and yet there are considerable slow-moving or obsolete inventories of these items. Nevertheless, how do we improve the SI from, let's say 15% to 45%, for example?

The basic rules of product line standardization

In a traditional sense, product standardization is a way to maintain consistency among the different iterations of a product or service across any given number of applications and markets. It also means that companies can sell different variations of the product or service without making extensive changes to fewer basic designs, only superficial modifications. Otherwise, the characteristics of the product remain uniform. The distinction here is that we want to use standardization as a platform to expand variety and growth (read scale), without adding excessive amounts of marginal costs. We want to be able to attract new customers and grow the long tail with a lot of less effort and cost.

As companies like Scania and Cummins would

prove, standardization and modularization are not incompatible with offering more choices to customers. By evolving the product line architecture and by governing complexity with 80/20 analytics, we can have all the traditional benefits of standardization, such as low cost and high quality, without having to sacrifice profitable variety.

The focus of product specification optimization (PSO) should be on cost, design, and new product development driven by the 80/20 analysis. The goal is to reduce the number of discrete products and parts, within a product line offering, consistently with the business strategy. PSO is not just about removing low-volume part numbers and SKUs. Nor it's about eliminating an entire business line from the company. PSO is about healing the products that remain after we rationalize the portfolio. Hence the reason why we must first streamline before we can standardize.

The first rule is to never leave eighty customers, or any strategic customer, without viable options to buy. Always offer alternatives to replace or reprice a product that needs changing, defining clear policies on tailored or customized products. How they should be priced and who should get them. If a freeloader product is in the mix, and repricing is not an option, managers need to improve margins by reducing cost or influencing the sales mix.

The second rule is not to allow PSO to be driven in isolation by a single area of the business, such as engineering, manufacturing, sales, or purchasing. When conducted in isolation, it quickly becomes ineffective. PSO is a multidisciplinary program and requires alignment among different functions to be successful. Small, multi-functional teams, working together under the guidance of a governing executive group, is the best way to get results. If possible, PSO needs participation and involvement from key customers and suppliers to succeed. The best results come when end-users and suppliers have a vested interest in addressing pain points that exist when doing business with the company.

The third rule is to connect PSO to the overall margin improvement work. If the company doesn't already have a managed pipeline of ideas and projects to improve margins, it should create one based on PSO. Never lose sight of the prize, which is to increase operating earnings while reducing the marginal cost of adding new products to the offering. It doesn't do any good to raise SI if we cannot improve return on sales. Managers also need to calibrate organizational expectations about the effort and time involved. PSO is not an overnight exercise and requires a dedicated team of insiders to do the work.

Lastly, to be sustainable, PSO needs a governing body and forum to filter new parts and products, deciding who should get them and how to make them available.

Regular screening is a critical element of governing complexity. Again, this is best accomplished when managers piggy-back on established management activities, such as new product introduction (NPI) and product management forums. The governing body should be able to control the entry gate to the portfolio by saying yes, no or "yes, but..." to new items, based on the data.

Simplifying the standardization process

Most companies arrive at standardization by necessity, embracing Lean to reduce waste and do more with less. Unfortunately, too many firms lose steam and get lost along the way of the Lean journey, because they fail to make the connection between value and complexity. Companies try to do too much, too fast and end up compounding the problem. Thus, the reason why 80/20 makes so much sense is that it puts the spotlight on what matters most, or on high and low-value areas of the portfolio in terms of margin and cost. When you focus on core customers, vendors and products, and physically segregate the eighty from the twenty, you make complexity cost (and waste) visible and have an extra incentive to do something about it.

PSO begins with 80/20 analytics applied to product structures and supply chains. We start by correlating SKUs to parts and parts to suppliers to gain insight on duplication, similarity, and material cost distribution. We link these datasets with the customer and product matrix, defining goals and improvement targets, keeping the value chain connected - from contribution margin to complexity cost. With the sharper focus provided by 80/20, we proceed to optimize product specifications and reduce part-count, lowering material cost per SKU. Then we turn our attention to the supply chain, leveraging purchase volumes, and collaborating with strategic suppliers to lower material cost per part or component.

Rather than tackling the entire portfolio at once, PSO focuses on the eighty or the high-value targets. Successful execution requires three elements. The first is the establishment of an agile, multidisciplinary team, capable of setting goals and implementing initiatives from start to finish. Second, the team needs data-rich and insightful analytics to select the most impactful projects (the eighty) to execute. Lastly, the working group must follow a systematic process to complete projects that can heal the portfolio and increase profitability. By doing so, they create a pipeline of ideas to be converted into profits.

Having the discipline to go through each phase methodically is essential to a successful program. The multidisciplinary team has three goals: set targets based on the analytics, design improvement initiatives, and implement the initiatives. In general, they spend 10% of the time analyzing and setting targets, 25% designing, planning, and detailing new actions, and 65% executing. The goal is to maintain a healthy pipeline, full of relevant ideas and initiatives, and keep them moving through the five levels of implementation or execution gates. The execution gates are the leading progress indicators and the standard steps for all initiatives.

5.2 The Steps (Gates) in the Project Pipeline

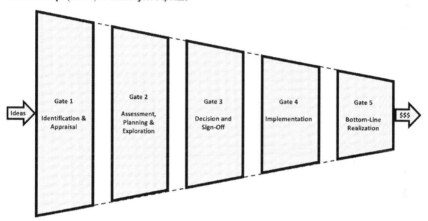

The first execution gate or the entry point to the pipeline is the identification and appraisal of initiatives derived from insights from 80/20 analytics. Data insights lead to ideas, which lead to actions. The team outlines the plans and provides rough estimates of the potential impact. Most ideas, at this point, come from data analysis workshops, after scrutinizing every quadrant. Gate number two is the assessment and planning phase. The team evaluates the initiatives and decides on whether to move them forward or not. Gate two is an exploratory phase, which usually demands additional analysis, data, and a dose of innovation. For instance, if a company decides that it needs to investigate the cost competitiveness of a core product, it will be conducting benchmarking and product teardowns versus competitors to validate the assumptions.

Gate number three is the commitment milestone and when the final decision to pursue the action is made. Here, it's imperative to have full backing from executive sponsors, finance, and other functional areas required to support the initiative. At this point, managers can have a pretty good idea of the profit improvement potential from the pipeline, based on projects that pass gate three. Gate four is the actual implementation phase and can be done internally by the team or outsourced to an external supplier. For example, if there is a need to modify a highly efficient assembly line to accommodate additional high-volume SKUs, we may want to involve technical resources from outside to come up with a plan and execute. More information on the actual execution methods will come later in this chapter. The last gate, or level five, is the bottom-line realization of the gains. Results are either brought to the P&L or fully verified by the company's controller.

Standardization analytics

80/20 analytics will help select the vital few SKUs, parts, commodities, and suppliers to examine in more detail. It will also help establish cost and diversification targets for products and components. Keep in mind that the main benefits from standardization will come from reductions in part count, harmonization of specs, and rationalization of suppliers.

Like we did with the offering, we can readily organize and connect the data concerning components and suppliers according to 80/20, placing it inside two separate grids. Keeping the same Pareto classification used for SKUs, based on contribution margin, we create two new matrices: one for SKUs versus components - the BOM matrix - and another for parts versus suppliers - the supplier matrix. We use total material cost spent on the period to classify parts and suppliers under the Pareto distribution. Where the increasing material cost reaches eighty percent of the total, we draw the two crossing lines creating the quadrants. At the intersection of SKU and component (and component and supplier), we enter the associated material cost and the number of units used or purchased during the period.

The purpose of organizing the data in such a way is to study the cost end of the hourglass, adding a few more layers to the analysis. Instead of contribution margin, used for the products and customers dataset, we use material cost as the bond between SKUs, components, and suppliers. Material cost is typically the most significant cost item within the contribution margin for manufacturing and distribution companies, just like labor cost is the critical item for service businesses.

5.3 The 80/20 Value Chain

The mere visualization of the size, shape, and density of the quads combined, provides a unique view of the entire value chain. The connection of the core areas of these three matrices embodies the zones where the company makes most of its money. As far as standardization goes, to have a positive effect on true profitability, we need to impact and heal the marginal products, components, and suppliers in these core areas while reducing the overall part count and proliferation everywhere else. That's why we use a microscope to pick the targets in Q1 and a telescope to select clusters of freeloaders and other items of interest in the other quads. While optimization efforts are critical to improving the competitiveness in the core zones, part count proliferation and complexity are pervasive problems across the portfolio.

While we can rationalize all other quadrants outside the core areas using pricing and simplification strategies, we should use more specialized tools and methods in Q3 to reduce part count and increase BOM similarity. In quad three, we also need to change the way we source components and design products using better design practices like design-for-manufacturing and assembly, for example. Engineering and purchasing will have to work together to create new standards and to foster better utilization of existing parts and suppliers.

The prime SKU targets in Q1 are those with low contribution margin, typically below the TrP target, for which increasing prices or replacing with other more profitable products are not viable options. Let's take a core product, for example, that you sell in high volumes to eighty customers at a competitive market price, but with a narrow margin. These types of SKUs are at the head of the demand curve and, to lift the company's profitability, you need to bring their margins upward. Situations like this require a higher level of attention and research, including a comparison against the best competitive products, to learn first-hand the gaps in cost, performance, and reliability.

Benchmarking is the activity of comparing targeted products versus the competition to learn everything you can, collecting ideas based on state of the art. Implementation teams organize workshops tearing down one or more competitive products, laying it all out on a workbench, hence benchmarking. You typically start with a price versus performance comparison, listing where you have feature gaps and advantages. You are exploring to learn about features, price points, competitive limitations, design characteristics, part count, materials, assembly processes, packaging, distribution channels, and so much more. Discoveries in a benchmarking study can give you new cost and performance references but can also influence the direction of your product design positively.

In parallel to benchmarking, the analysis team determines the clean sheet target costing (CSTC) for the product. CSTC is a bottom-up study designed to evaluate the cost of each component or service throughout the entire value chain, using available data sources for materials, labor, energy, and other production inputs. The primary objective is to obtain the "should cost" figure for a product so we can establish reduction targets. Clean sheet costing also helps with new design and manufacturing improvement ideas since it delves into the primary sources of the product cost. By knowing the "should cost," we can better negotiate with suppliers and have a measurable understanding of the implications when changing product sources.

We must also determine the total cost of ownership or TCO for items purchased by the company, which is the real cost of procuring a component or a service from the supply chain. This metric is the component equivalent of true profitability and is an assessment device used by buyers to reflect all the direct and indirect costs associated with a commodity or a finished product. Multidisciplinary teams (purchasing, engineering, and finance) arrive at TCO by gathering data and creating value stream maps, defining cost areas that are relevant to the purchasing process.

If the company is buying a vehicle, for example, the cost elements of TCO might include the purchase price, the operating cost, and the maintenance or repair cost. Each business needs to decide what goes in the TCO of any critical component or product. For example, to own a car, a company must maintain it, keep it registered and licensed, insure it, and repair it when it breaks down. On the other hand, to buy a component from an overseas supplier, the buyer must consider the purchase price, currency implications, duties, freight, and inventory carrying costs to compensate for the extended supply chain. Even if a product doesn't seem to have a recurring cost associated with it, you still have a storage fee if you need to keep it in a warehouse.

However, how do we select the SKUs and parts to apply CSTC and TCO? Quadrant one and the transitional zone in quadrant three are the priorities. Work teams choose every SKU that does not meet the TrP threshold, with their respective components and suppliers in these areas. The customer versus product matrix is the starting point. During insight gathering sessions, we first determine high-value target SKUs for conducting benchmarking and CSTC exercises. The outcome of these activities, coupled with the 80/20 BOM and supplier data, will point to the high-value parts from a TCO perspective. The remaining regions, outside of quad one and transitional zone, are less productive when choosing individual targets for cost optimization.

When it comes to tackling part count reduction, we change the focus from individual items to groups and families of products. The BOM similarity index (SI) decomposes the bill of materials and its nested hierarchy to determine the similar components that make-up the entire offering or a subset of products. SI is used to assess the underlying product complexity but also to learn a component's usage and spread across the portfolio. It creates similarity groupings by arranging the parts in three distinct categories: exact match (differ only at a superficial level by packaging or labeling, for example), same components (differing quantities but the equal basic parts) and similar (above 80% of the same elements).

SI is especially suitable when looking for standardization targets within the same business unit, manufacturing plant, or supply chain. While there are no absolute standards to say if an SI of 32%, for example, is good or bad, this metric helps to compare the level of complexity between market segments and product families. The overall company SI can be used as a KPI to determine how much standardization or complexity is present in the offering. SI also helps to flag and segregate critical components for more in-depth analysis and is the best indicator for standardization progress and internal complexity cost.

From a part count reduction perspective, we want to single out products with unique components and low SI. There is always the potential to increase margins by replacing unique and different parts for standard ones and leveraging high-volume components across other products. We also want to look closer at supporting products that are sold almost exclusively to core customers, since they point to customer-induced proliferation.

By applying SI to each core product family, we find that companies typically sell high-volume products to two or more customers for the same application with radically different bills of materials and very different supply chains. Other times, data will show that competing customers buy very distinct mixes of supporting products for the same use. One of the worst killers of profitability is an unfavorable mix of low-volume products which are custom built to support the needs of core customers. There's always money to be made by using more standard products and parts and supply chain. The peeling of the SKU data combined with the similarity index will lead us to product families, market segments, and customers that could benefit from increased standardization.

Product Specification Optimization (PSO)

Product standardization boosts profitability by optimizing the design and controlling portfolio variety. We want to lower the cost per unit of components and reduce part count and proliferation across the board. PSO requires teamwork and a good dose of innovation, built on insights from 80/20 analytics and competitive analysis. As discussed, very few companies measure the level of duplication and proliferation in their parts database. This indifferent attitude is because, in general, organizations do not understand the implications of excessive part propagation. Saying that complexity avoidance is everyone's responsibility is the same as saying that no one is accountable for it. Engineers are, for the most part, happy to reuse existing components, but the lack of standards, systems, and data to facilitate the work makes it harder to execute. From the engineer's perspective, using a new part doesn't cost anything.

Typically, purchasing is involved in different degrees during the design process, but, once the BOM is released and the procurement work starts, it's tricky to change the design. The cost of qualifying and developing new suppliers can be high. Manufacturing also sees the proliferation from their end but eliminating duplicate parts require changes to orders and equipment, which cost money and needs time.

Part of the solution is to make everyone aware of the problem by measuring complexity and creating a governing process that promotes communication and collaboration between all affected areas across the entire lifecycle of a product. The other critical element is to adapt the existing design methodology to one that promotes greater standardization and modularity going forward. The governing process gives us a forum and the analytical mechanism to foster reuse of parts while the new design approach yields lower cost and simplicity from the start.

When similarity levels in the product structure are too low, companies must focus on design-for-simplicity first. Design-for-variety should come only when the business is ready to govern complexity. Even if we can only reduce part count going forward, on new products, the benefits are still worth the effort, considering how fast the portfolio changes in the complexity zone.

Design-for-simplicity reduces the part count by simplifying the ways by which products are manufactured or assembled. Only after addressing extreme variation, companies can move forward to a new product line architecture and use design-for-variety to expand the long tail and grow with less cost. 80/20 thinking is critical when designing-for-simplicity since part count reduction relies on replacing as many single-uses, low-volume parts (twenty) with a combination of high-volume (eighty), multipurpose, and manufacturing-friendly components.

The best design-for-simplicity methods combine the redesign of existing products, via a zero-based design mindset, with another approach known as DFMA or design for manufacturing and assembly. Zero-based design is a method by which we reduce the part count of a target product to zero and then add back only the essential components to match the desired functionality and features. In the final analysis, a product is nothing more than a "job to be done." As Clayton Christensen[x] says, "the job is what the customer is trying to accomplish," and in most cases, companies can use different solutions, components, and even other products to get the job done. Hence, whenever rethinking a product from scratch, we must keep in mind what the customer is trying to do, how the competition is addressing the need and what else we already have in our pockets that we can use to solve the problem.

As we rebuild the product, we strive to employ the highest possible number of eighty parts and components that have extensive usage across the portfolio. We are always better off using a variant of an eighty part, which is built in a high-volume line or supplied by an eighty vendor, rather than using a twenty part from a low-volume source. When there is a need to add a low-volume part, we first attempt to use standard and multipurpose components before resorting to a unique one. The goal is to eliminate or reduce as many low-usage, custom-made, and specialty parts as possible, such as those made with exotic materials.

DFMA is a design method that makes it easy for purchasing and manufacturing to produce something most efficiently and economically. DFMA is useful because if forces engineering to promote simplicity and standardization by creating a direct connection between part count and the cost of sourcing and manufacturing. On average, design choices account for about 70% of the manufacturing cost, while production decisions are responsible for only 20%. A reduction in the number of parts is the best opportunity to decrease product cost. It's like a positive chain reaction impacting engineering time, fewer vendors, fewer purchases, specialized equipment, quality inspection, and warranty expenses.

From a pure manufacturing standpoint, there are different ways to increase standardization and reduce part count. Additive manufacturing uses technologies that build three-dimensional parts by adding layer-upon-layer of material. A growing number of manufacturers are adopting this technology. For instance, automotive OEMs use 3D metal printing to produce medium-to-high volume service parts that go in vehicles launched 15 to 20 years ago. Daimler is an example of a company that takes advantage of additive manufacturing to make complex spare parts using 3D metal printing. The quality is excellent, and they can be produced on-demand, reducing the need to forecast production volume and to stock them.

Flexible production technologies like additive manufacturing are increasingly important, but the design is still the most critical factor in this equation. Simplicity and modularity are very impactful when built into the architecture of the product from the beginning. Early involvement and teamwork with procurement and manufacturing are essential, and engineers need a simultaneous and collaborative process combined with analytical tools to make optimal design decisions.

Teams work on part count reduction using zero-based design to decrease the number of discrete items, by standardizing around eighty or preferred components. They start by asking a simple question: What is the minimum list of part types we need to create this product? Primed with clean sheet costing and the benchmarking data, they reconstruct the product simplifying the BOM and replacing low use with standard parts along the way. A standard part is one that is not custom-made and is highly available. Preferably engineers make use of commercial off-the-shelf (COTS) items whenever available since their cost, availability, and reliability are well known. Some standard COTS items include fasteners, motors, gears, seals, pins and springs.

Another class of parts we strive to apply during zero-based design are multipurpose components, which can be both multi-functional and multi-use. Multi-functional components can work in varied ways, for example, a bolt that can be part of a structure and dissipate heat at the same time. A multi-use item is mostly used across products to facilitate a manufacturing or assembly process. They usually reduce cost by decreasing labor and capital expenditures. For instance, using an existing low-volume housing for which we have already invested in the manufacturing tooling.

DFMA is not exclusive to new projects and should be employed to redesign existing products from a zero-based standpoint. Manufacturing or assembly-friendly parts include pieces that are easy to fabricate, easy to assemble, and require minimum handling during the production process. They help reduce direct and indirect labor costs, capital expenditures, improve quality, and increase throughput. As a rule, engineers should minimize the use of fasteners and replace them for tabs or snap-fit parts whenever possible. If you must use nuts and bolts, for example, you will want to use standard, COTS fasteners and of similar size to reduce the need for special assembly equipment. Being assembly-friendly also means that you should maximize compliance to avoid errors during production. Reduce variances in part dimensions and tolerances and build in assembly-proof features whenever possible, such as chamfers and guides. Engineers should prioritize symmetry in designs, to avoid mistakes in the orientation of the parts. If design symmetry is not possible, then asymmetry must be exaggerated to prevent failures.

From a high-level view, the entire process of creating lucrative and smart variety starts when managers define complexity objectively and set goals based on true profitability. Standardization is an essential step towards modular design. The following table depicts the stages and approaches to introduce profitable variety.

5.4 Designing Products for Simplicity and Variety

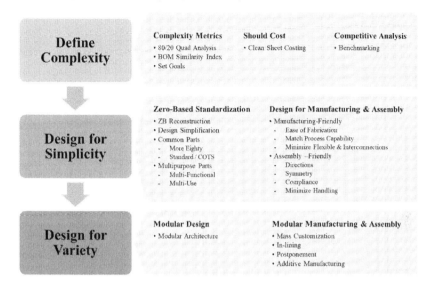

During implementation, multifunctional teams (engineering, purchasing, manufacturing, and quality), armed with 80/20 analytics and design for simplicity tools, attack complexity, and proliferation where it matters. The missing ingredient to optimize the offering is a dose of innovation, which we will discuss after this example related to the automotive industry.

Lessons from the passenger car industry

No other industry can benefit as much as the automotive industry when it comes to part count reduction and simplification. The passenger car and commercial vehicle businesses are very challenging. We have everything going on at the same time - model proliferation, electrification, changes in consumer patterns, driverless vehicles, continued globalization, new entrants, environmental pressures, and the slow death of the aftermarket. The automotive industry is fertile ground for a remaking of itself.

However, it will take time and brute force to change most car giants from cost-cutters into masters of complexity. Standardization, part count reduction, and additive manufacturing are just some of the change agents, and they also happen to be pillars of the so-called Industry 4.0, which is the name given to the trend of increasing automation and data exchange in production. Additive manufacturing is accelerating part count reduction and modularization, and it's likely to help further destroy the aftermarket business in the car industry.

Indeed, there are very few masters of complexity in the automotive world (Scania, on the truck side, being one of them). However, Toyota, the precursor and the master of all Lean practitioners, is working hard to simplify itself. After the 2008 economic crisis, complexity became unbearable for Toyota. The company held as many as 100 vehicle platforms and sub-platforms in its global offering and more than 800 power trains. This level of proliferation was unprecedented and painful for a company with such a strong focus on eliminating waste and raising productivity. After the crisis, it created an aggressive standardization and modularization program, named TNGA for Toyota New Global Architecture[xi].

TNGA was about increasing reuse of parts and modularity, but it was also about changing the way the company designed its products. Toyota focused on design-for-simplicity using DFMA, and adopting concurrent design and development of multiple models, making extensive use of standard modular components. Toyota launched the first cars from this program in 2015, in the form of three front-wheel-drive platforms, which represented about half of the company's global production. As an ongoing effort, TNGA should increase product development efficiency by 20 to 30 percent and communize about 70 to 80 percent of the parts across the portfolio. The prediction is that cars developed under TNGA will share 20 to 30 percent of their components. The Toyota hybrid and plug-in-hybrid Prius was one of the first vehicles designed under the new common platforms.

On the electrification front, it's fascinating to watch the battle between new electric-vehicle entrants like Tesla and Nikola against industry giants like Toyota, VW, Daimler, BMW, Ford, and GM, for example - if you are in the spectator's chair. Industry analysts believe that the future of cars is "electric, autonomous and shared." The electric prediction is quickly becoming a reality as new models enter the market every day, and the total cost of ownership of battery-electric vehicles (BEV) keeps falling.

One of the significant reasons why TCO is coming down is that electric cars, such as the Tesla Model 3, have significantly fewer parts when compared with the internal combustion engine (ICE) vehicles. Tesla says its drivetrain has about 17 moving parts compared with about 200 in a conventional internal combustion drivetrain[xii]. Reliability gets a boost, due to low part count while operating and maintenance costs drop. BEVs are also a lot more energy-efficient, emit lower emissions, and are safer than ICEs.

While Tesla develops BEVs from a clean sheet of paper, other carmakers like GM, adapted existing designs to create the Chevy Bolt, for instance. The vehicle, developed by GM's South Korea arm, was engineered around a large 60-kWh LG battery pack, which provides structural integrity[xiii]. No doubt the Chevy Bolt is a competitive BEV. However, one can only imagine the advantage that Tesla has, by affording to design an entire vehicle from scratch. GM, BMW, Nissan, and Toyota, to name a few, will have to innovate and simplify at the same time, while Tesla and other entrants will prey on the complexity created by its competitors, in terms of models, design, production, and distribution.

Too much complexity can limit growth and profitability, as in Toyota's case. Simplification and standardization help heal the portfolio and retake growth. However, built-in simplicity and modularity can be incredibly disruptive and beneficial, especially when the other market players have become complacent with the profitless kind of variety.

Simplicity-focused innovation

Peter Drucker once said that "the business has only two functions – marketing and innovation." While most companies have well-developed marketing, the majority struggle to innovate. The focus of manufacturing and distribution companies is more on product development and less on systematic innovation. They solve problems using trial-and-error and rely on flashes of inspiration to generate new ideas.

At the heart of the issue is that organizations have a hard time identifying and solving the right problems. They become self-centered and consumed by an excessive number of projects, resorting to offering proliferation in response to market changes and competitive pressures. Successful companies, in contrast, are always solving problems by adapting existing solutions first and are judicious before adding new SKUs and features. They center on customer's pain points and use data analysis to select the vital few programs. The result is a small but healthy and relevant pipeline of projects aimed at portfolio optimization.

Product line standardization focuses on design and cost, but it also relies on innovation to come up with new ideas directed at simplifying the offering. It begins with 80/20 analytics and uses workshops to produce concepts and solve problems related to design optimization. Successful PSO is customer-centric and capable of identifying solutions that satisfy the current application range and address key pain points. It's a collaborative endeavor, but it's also not an overnight exercise. There are many ways to conduct PSO workshops, but the most effective ones seem always to rely on three steps: divergence, exploration, and convergence.

Diverging or fanning is the first phase when you promote the diversity of thought, inspired by the data and the insights. To work well, teams must clearly define and quantify the problem before they start - a problem clearly stated is a problem half solved. Once the group understands the problem, several tools can be applied to help identify causal factors and create a solution path, such as Five-Whys and Cause and Effect Diagrams, for example.

The use of 80/20 analytics ensures that you are mining for problems to solve in the right places. Look first at the core and use the lessons learned from benchmarking, clean-sheet costing, and TCO exercises to come up with a shortlist of pain points to address. Establish a framework to think about the relevance of the ideas without pre-judgment. Teams reach convergence when they arrive at a joint and prioritized list of potential solutions. The next step is to test and explore the leading concepts.

Depending on the nature of the problem, there are a variety of exploration methods available, such as prototyping or piloting, for example. However, most of the time, exploration means testing ideas carefully for applicability and financial viability before spending too much time evolving the concept. It also means talking to customers, suppliers, and internal experts early on to obtain their viewpoints. For instance, if the idea consists of using a more cost-effective material across several SKUs, the new material cost data should be entered in the analytical model to confirm its impact.

After selecting one or two potential ideas, teams will further evolve and refine the chosen concepts during the convergence phase, using more specialized tools. Start with what you've learned from the exploration, analytics, and benchmarking to guide the solution. Ensure that the team possesses first-hand knowledge and subject matter expertise available on the issue, bringing data along from the exploration phase. Logical ideation tools like flow charts and affinity diagrams can help structure the data and retain lessons learned, allowing the team to learn more about the problem. Here's an example of an affinity diagram linking the three 80/20 matrices for a few SKUs.

5.5 Example of Affinity Diagram

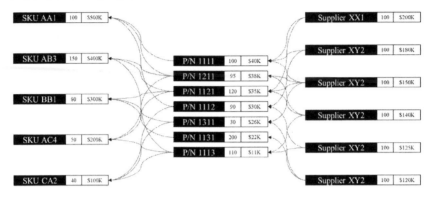

During convergence, apply a combination of new and lateral thinking and avoid reinventing the wheel. In most cases, the solution is to adapt or to refine something that the company or the customer is already doing. Take time to choose more than one problem-solving technique and train everyone on these tools before using them. An example of a more generic, lateral thinking tool is TRIZ[xiv], developed by Altshuller and others, from the former USSR, between 1946 and 1985. TRIZ accelerates a project team's ability to solve problems creatively by helping them go back and forth between divergent and convergent thinking based on logic, data, and research.

The TRIZ method considers two universal principles of creativity: first, somebody, sometime, somewhere has already solved your problem or one like it. Creativity means finding that solution and adapting it.

Secondly, don't accept contradictions. Resolve them. Problems and solutions repeat themselves across industries and sciences, as well as the patterns of technical evolution. To learn more about TRIZ and experiment with how it can help resolve problems, you can look at *www.triz40.com*. The website allows you to study practical rules on how to solve contradictions, such as reducing the complexity of a device while maintaining its functionality.

Samsung is an excellent example of an innovative company that uses TRIZ, despite recent setbacks and some criticism that its success is mostly due to copying and tweaking the innovation of others. However, the reality is, Samsung is a global leader in many different product categories, different than Apple and Google, for example. A 2016 article by Haydn Shaughnessy on Forbes Magazine shows how TRIZ has become a significant innovation engine for growth and market leadership at Samsung.

"TRIZ has become the bedrock of innovation at Samsung. Moreover, it was introduced at Samsung by Russian engineers whom Samsung had hired into its Seoul Labs in the early 2000s. In 2003 TRIZ led to 50 new patents for Samsung, and in 2004 one project alone, a DVD pick-up innovation saved Samsung over 100 million dollars. TRIZ is now an essential skill set if you want to advance within Samsung."

As we solve problems to increase the usage of high-volume components and drive similarity across the BOMs, we start shifting focus to the supply chain. We go from product to part or commodity and deep dive on ways to reduce the cost of these items via optimizing the supply base.

Supply Chain Optimization

Virtually all companies have gaps between the planned and the actual cost of products and components. Once a product is approved, the targeted design cost turns into a theoretical reference point to achieve since complexity is always working against the target. On top of the sub-optimal project and design choices, we experience cost degradation from poor supplier selection and other unexpected supply chain charges. The reality is that, once a component leaves the design desk, sourcing is the primary factor in product cost overruns.

Product standardization and part count reduction programs can reduce a portion of the cost gap. However, to get closer to the theoretical target, managers need to rethink the supply chain strategy for the eighty components. The starting point is to assess the level of alignment between the value chain and the supply chain. Then we need to determine how much we should pay for each core product, part, or service. 80/20 vendor analytics, clean-sheet costing, and TCO analysis are used to answer these two essential questions. Do we have the best supplier network focused on our eighty products? What should we pay for the eighty components?

The goals of supply chain optimization or SCO are to lower the total cost of ownership, or the landed cost per unit, and to synchronize the supply chain for maximum effectiveness. We achieve TCO reduction by leveraging scale and collaborating with core suppliers. Supply chain synchronization is essential to give buyers additional clout and negotiating power. Buyers also need to accumulate useful insight into suppliers, markets, and commodities to create and use leverage.

To build leverage is to change the balance of power and to elevate the relationship with every core vendor, from transactional to strategic. We accomplish that by consolidating purchasing dollars on fewer strategic suppliers, assessing make versus buy opportunities and creating rules-based procurement to purchase standard parts and services. To collaborate is to work closely with strategic suppliers, increasing logistical and productive efficiencies for both companies, sharing information, and participating in cost reduction programs, including PSO workshops.

Like the way we look at customers, not all suppliers are equal. We should rearrange the vendor and

SKU matrix to reflect the optimized reality, based on where the supplier falls in the value chain. However, before we start consolidating volumes and negotiating prices, we need two additional pieces of insight. First, we need to attribute a supply risk factor to each component in quadrants one and three. Supply risk is high when we are dealing with rare materials and those that are subject to volatility in global markets. We can say, for example, that petroleum-based resin prices are volatile, considering how much fluctuation there is in oil prices.

Second, we need to know everything we can about the existing and future strategic suppliers, including how much power they have in the industry, as well as how much power we have with them. One way to do this analysis is to use Porter's Five Forces[xv]. Another way is to use big-data analytics to search the internet for non-structured information on markets, commodities, and suppliers. Companies can learn a lot by merely visualizing the web traffic created for a supplier, for example. Public company's websites, chat rooms, regulatory news, and customer reviews, for example, can provide ample indications about a supplier reputation and power in the industry.

The easiest way to redefine the relationship with your core suppliers is to provide additional value, awarding them with attractive businesses, such as high-profit, high-volume, and low-risk supply. Based on the rearranged supplier matrix, we look for opportunities to create negotiation leverage by offering additional value. You want to consolidate the supply chain of your eighty parts with your eighty suppliers, considering the profit impact (volume and margin) and the supply risk (market price volatility and complicated logistics, for example). Keep in mind that, whenever possible, we should always have a second or third alternative for strategic suppliers, mainly for items with high supply risk. We can look at untapped industry players or new entrants in adjacent markets, for example. We should also consider insourcing an eighty, high-risk component if we can't identify viable alternatives.

We will find many small and low-volume vendors at the bottom of the matrix, below the transitional area in Q3, with different degrees of risk. Not unlikely the way we mark strategic customers and baby-whales, we need to identify potential core suppliers and the ones that present a higher risk. High-risk suppliers in this area are also called bottlenecks. We should apply purchasing power and leverage to procure low supply risk components and start reducing the number of low-value suppliers.

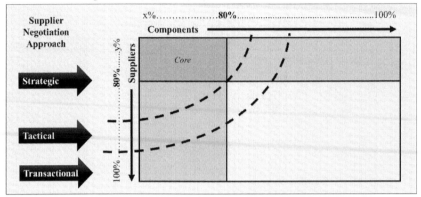

Product line standardization helps reduce the number of bottleneck suppliers by minimizing the existence of high-risk items in the BOM, substituting them for standard and COTS components. For the remaining bottleneck items, purchasing must spread the risk by engaging new suppliers and finding ways to control the existing ones. Typical approaches used to buy these items include overordering and carrying some buffer inventory for contingencies.

For the tactical and transactional areas in the picture above, we should use a combination of direct and rules-based procurement. Rules-based is the precursor to a marketplace maker, for companies that wish to buy both components and finished products online. Such initiatives are known as procurement auctions or reverse auctions and can be used to expand the long tail. The company uses its online portal or a third-party market maker to procure any part that has low supply risk and is non-critical.

Typically, the buyer issues an RFP (request for proposal) on the auction site for a group of products or services. Potential suppliers will input their quotes, and the buyer will award a supplier contract to the bidder of their choosing. Companies use broader criteria, other than the lowest price, to pick the winning supplier. Reverse auctions are the fastest and most efficient ways to buy low-risk commodities or to outsource components and finished products. They also significantly lower the cost per transaction, compared to the direct procurement process.

Standardization and rules-based procurement will foster the realignment, streamline the supply base, and lower the cost per transaction for purchasing. Beyond these actions and along the same lines of customer divestment, companies should have a process to manage attrition and reduce the number of direct suppliers. As we know by now, most businesses spend most of their cost of goods sold with only a small number of suppliers. The remaining small vendors or the twenty, typically consume more than 50% of the purchasing organization's time and resources.

Supplier consolidation reduces overhead by lowering both direct and indirect purchasing costs. Once companies realign the supplier network with their core products and customers, they can scrutinize the different families or categories of SKUs to condense the number of vendors by product class, always considering the risk involved. By synchronizing supply base and high-value products, companies realize an increase in purchasing power and become less vulnerable to sourcing issues. It allows purchasing to develop a closer relationship with the few core suppliers. Like part count reduction, supply chain optimization is an ongoing process to allow buyers to focus on the strategic suppliers.

Finally, SCO is a crucial strategy to be used within the project pipeline to heal the portfolio. Combining product specification and supply chain optimization is a very effective way to reduce both complexity and direct material cost. They work together and have minimal or no dependency on pricing to raise true profitability. While they take longer to implement, they produce longer-lasting results than pricing alone. Here's a complete view of the process based on the execution gates.

5.7 The Project Pipeline and the Tools Used at Each Stage

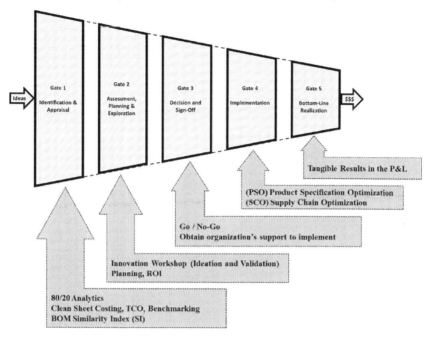

The PSO and SCO pipelines, together with new product introduction (NPI) and product management, are typically sum of all management processes used to govern portfolio complexity in the company. They are completely interdependent and require data from inside and outside the business to function correctly. Product planning and NPI deal with the future offering, while product management and PSO/SCO pipelines deal with the present status of the portfolio. Systematic governance is essential for managing the long tail in such a way that we can execute on the type of expansion that limits complexity and excessive overhead.

6 SMART VARIETY

Up to this point, we have discussed how to streamline the long tail and lift true profitability by healing products and optimizing supply chains. This stage is about expanding the portfolio to grow revenues and profits, using the long tail as a means to attract new customers and benefit from low-volume SKUs, while maintaining simplicity and minimizing overhead. The picture below shows the three essential phases to lift true profitability and retake growth of the offering.

6.1. Boosting True Profitability

While companies restore SKU growth immediately after streamlining the portfolio, they usually go through a standardization phase (healing), before they focus on smart variety. However, as businesses expand, they must keep working on these three fronts simultaneously, to govern complexity. The work needs gradual involvement from different functions and people in the organization, until the point where everyone understands and supports the idea of managing-for-variety.

Smart variety can be used to describe many types of diversification strategies, but in our case, it refers to how you make products available in your portfolio. First, are products that have the highest levels of similarity with the eighty products and components in your offering. Second, smart variety can also denote a collection of SKUs that are not made by your company but outsourced to core suppliers and sold to your customers, under the same or different brands. The first type of product, or the one using high-volume components, should have higher levels of true profitability. The second type, or the ones you outsource, should represent a known quantity concerning the total cost of ownership (TCO). Both types of smart variety are needed to make money with the long tail. To illustrate the concept, let's take a look at Seiko, the vertically integrated watch manufacturer.

Seiko is an iconic Japanese watchmaker offering thousands of watch SKUs around the world. The company was founded roughly 140 years ago and is responsible for some of the most significant technical and commercial innovations in the very competitive and brand prolific watch business. For instance, Seiko was one of the first companies to release a quartz timepiece, which nearly brought the mechanical watch competitors from Switzerland to their knees. Today, Seiko produces large quantities of mechanical, quartz, solar and kinetic watches under different brands (Seiko, Presage, Credor, and Grand Seiko), with price points ranging from US$45 to US$550,000.

One of the commendable things about Seiko is how successfully they manage product variety and complexity using standardization and modularity to compete in a market that values unique designs and limited editions. For instance, the low-priced Seiko 5 watch, released in 1963, is a huge global success and embodies the design principles used by the company to attain variation in unique designs, low cost, and bulletproof quality. The watch design characteristics served the needs of the 1960's generation, who were more concerned about practicality and value. Seiko 5 has five essential design attributes that came from carefully reading into spoken and unspoken customer pain points. The company later applied these five principles into hundreds of different watches:

1. Automatic winding
2. Day/date displayed in a single window
3. Water resistance
4. Recessed crown at the 4 o'clock position
5. Durable steel case and bracelet

To balance variation and cost, Seiko uses only a handful of different movements or watch mechanisms to produce an enormous number of different designs. For example, for mechanical watches, Seiko has no more than ten calibers which, combined with a large number of exterior designs and components, produce a great variety of different SKUs. Calibers are the expensive components of mechanical watches, applied to both eighty and twenty products to increase reuse and similarity.

The company fully understands the power of innovation and product diversification in the offering. The variety of choices, ubiquity, and modularity in Seiko's product line is a powerful customer magnet. Nevertheless, Seiko also profits from this variety and modularity in the aftermarket, by encouraging customers to thinker with the external design and looks of the watch, while selling modification parts. The practice has become so prevalent that there are vast numbers of followers around the world known as Seiko modders. "The idea can be simple: take a Seiko watch, pull it apart, and swap in a different dial, maybe some hands from a different watch, to customize its look. Modders have explored these design refurbishments and thousands of others for years thanks to a right eye and an impressive Seiko part inventory."[xvi]

Through innovation and standardization of components and design principles, Seiko keeps expanding the long tail of its offering while maintaining complexity and overhead costs under control. The company proves that manufacturers can diversify into multiple brands and price points to attract new buyers, without succumbing to chaos. Managing-for-variety requires unconventional marketing and product management processes, capable of mastering and governing complexity. Seiko is a master of complexity, and for several decades now, the company has adapted its business model to design, produce, and sell the smart kind of variety.

Design-for-variety is very powerful and enables a business to offer multiple variants of a product line with minimum cost and effort. However, to master complexity like Seiko, companies must go beyond the design method and adopt the other disciplines of managing-for-variety (MFV), as depicted in the picture below.

6.2 Disciplines Involved in Managing for Variety

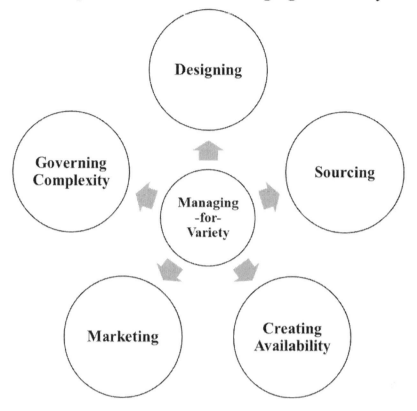

Each of the above elements holds different management practices associated with them, and new concepts appear every day, fueled by the digital transformation. In design-for-variety, for instance, we have solutions that embed standardization principles in the design tools, connecting with the BOM database to foster reuse and switchability. We also have the growing adoption of additive manufacturing, allowing for mass customization. We also have new big-data analytics and cloud visualization tools to help manage all this.

Masters of complexity, like Seiko and Amazon, are experts in all five MFV disciplines. Their economic performance is a direct consequence of managing complexity and having a business model that ensures true profitability of products and services. Traditional financial analysis often misses the competitive advantage of mastering complexity. As we discuss each discipline, the intention is not to exhaust the MFV topics but to provide an executive overview that lets managers embrace the idea and explore solutions.

Designing-for-variety (DFV)

DFV is an approach to reduce internal variation and complexity while increasing the company's ability to respond to external customer demands for variants and made-to-order products. The challenge is to minimize the complexity and overhead costs without reducing the scope and breadth of the offering. We want to create flexible product line architectures and product platforms that allow for the introduction of multiple SKUs, based mainly on the same elements.

Seiko's 6R15 mechanical caliber is an eighty component or assembly, designated as a platform in a modular product line, applied to many different models of watches across the offering. By using the 6R15 to power high and low-volume timepieces, Seiko achieves large economies of scale and true profitability. The determining features for each platform are the types of chronological complications (day, date, chronograph, and reserve indication for example) and the number of vibrations per hour (21,600, 28,800 or 36,000). Each movement, in the small lineup of mechanical calibers, is a unique platform from a functionality standpoint. Therefore, there are no two movements with the same functionality within each brand.

Similar to standardization, modularity does not require turning the business upside down to revamp all its product families at the same time. That is too risky. The best approach is to apply DFV going forward, to new and modified products, based on the product launching strategy and roadmap. The benefits of increasing modularity will become evident as the business starts reusing more high-volume components and platforms, during standardization. Once there is critical mass around the eighty platforms, the company will eventually decide to rethink the architecture of the existing offering, considering the benefits of a modular design. Modularity requires critical mass to take hold.

In general, there are five steps to DFV. The first one is the definition of goals, examining the current levels of BOM similarity, and deciding on how much improvement is needed. Next step is to analyze the product line in regards to variation objectives and determine how many and which modules are required. Like the Seiko lineup of mechanical movements (complications and number of beats per hour), we need to be clear about the function or job to be done by each module. We decompose the product into the desired functions and determine which and how many platforms are necessary to perform each task. Although each module will carry unique functionality, ideally we want to be able to use or tweak an existing eighty module or component to get the job done.

The third step is the requirements classification, where we list all the essential characteristics and the predicted impact they will have on the product. We need to determine who is behind each requirement, i.e., if the demand for the variant characteristic comes from the customer (external) or the company itself (internal). The goal is to reduce the variety and the inherent complexity that is created by the company to a minimum. The fourth step is the development of alternative solutions. This stage is where the designer conceives the product line architecture or the multiple ways and the rules to put the modules together and create a series of product variants.

The final step is to evaluate the modular solution concerning its ability to produce variety from only a few essential elements. The question here is whether the architecture devised will deliver the number and the types of SKUs that will allow us to do the job for the customer, and to expand the portfolio using high-value platforms and components. DFV is a combination of best practices in product strategy and design. All of the best practices used during standardization are applicable here. However, the critical difference is that we are trying to decompose the "jobs to be done" in clear chunks or modules.

Designers should use the following principles for DFV[xvii]. Below is a list of guidelines and examples.

Guideline	*Example*
• Assign **every function** and variant characteristic directly **to one module** of the product.	*Decompose each function and variant characteristic into a module.*
• **Changing one product characteristic** should **not affect more than one module**.	*A function of the above.*
• Use as many **standard parts** as possible.	*Use only one spring part number, capable of taking the force applied to multiple parts.*
• Standardize **design parameters** of	*Geometry and materials – how*

multiple variants.	*different parts interface with other elements or modules.*
• Use **overdesign** to avoid different parts.	*Use a larger-capacity part across the entire product line.*
• Use **higher symmetry** to generate geometric product variants.	*Use an additional interface between two elements to create multiple parts.*
• Use **software and hardware solutions** to create product variants.	*To be able to combine multiple devices into one.*
• Design **compatible module interfaces**.	*The LEGO approaches.*
• Use **parallel and serial configurations** to create performance variants.	*Use similar batteries instead of different ones with different voltages.*
• **Decompose** cost-intensive components with many variants to	*Use one computer frame with multiple*

standard components. *external adapters versus many different frames.*

- Use **cut to fit modularity** to create geometric variants. *Use a machine tool extension that enables using the same device for multiple parts.*

- Use **additional elements** to create geometric variants. *Use a product extension that allows for new application or functionality.*

- Isolate variant **characteristics with no function** into new cost-efficient components. *Uncouple appearance, color, and other cosmetic factors from the actual feature set of a device.*

An excellent example of a company that uses modular design to gain a competitive advantage is Scania, the global truck manufacturer, based in Sweden. Scania prides itself on a modular system that provides customers with multiple options and configurations. Their engineering offices and plants are not subject to unmanageable amounts of complexity: they use a limited number of building blocks with many variations. Scania products share components across a wide range of vehicles and applications.

For example, all of Scania's truck cabs, regardless of size, have the same interface with the chassis. All engines and gearboxes have the same mounting points on the chassis, irrespective of size. The chassis, in turn, is built up by a large number of frame components that fit together in countless combinations. Scania laid the groundwork for modularization more than fifty years ago and has been refining the system ever since.

We cannot underestimate the impact of reducing part count and SKU numbers, as described in this paragraph from the AME article "The Spirit in the Walls: A Pattern for High Performance at Scania"[xviii]:

"Everyone believes that a manufacturer will improve costs and profitability by reducing the number of different parts in its products. Also, for a good reason. With fewer different parts, less effort and resources are required to design, make, and service a product line. Accordingly, activity-based cost management systems routinely use part number count as a cost driver to estimate how much financial performance will improve by reducing the number of different parts. However, it is not well understood that cost-driver information may capture only a small fraction of the financial improvement that part-number austerity makes possible."

Sourcing products for the long tail

The more a business wishes to grow an attractive and lucrative long tail, the more determined it needs to be in outsourcing its low-volume products. At the same time, it must be prepared to continuously expand the portfolio with novel and relevant products and services supplied by outside vendors. To strengthen the tail, successful companies maintain a healthy flow of SKUs capable of appealing to new customers and making money from a true profitability standpoint.

Masters of complexity create availability and diversification using beneficial variety. They invest in a type of sourcing capability which is different from traditional purchasing or the activity to procure components to feed the production line; they focus on partnering with expert suppliers and developing a broader and more efficient commercial ecosystem. Rather than seeing outsourcing as a make-versus-buy dilemma, they see outsourcing as an opportunity to liberate resources from handling complexity to work on growth initiatives.

The notion of more suppliers and partnering with new vendors seem to fly in the face of supply chain rationalization, discussed in the last chapter. Indeed, there are significant cost-savings from streamlining vendors and optimizing the purchase of tail components used for in-house products. However, two critical differences make sourcing for the long tail dissimilar. First, when we buy finished products from outside, instead of making them ourselves, we are reducing part count and overhead from design, procurement, production, and support. Second, we are using a commercial ecosystem, such as a virtual marketplace, which leaves the complexity burden entirely with the supplier.

To keep the long tail provided, we need a combination of proprietary and generic SKUs. The central idea is to compose the tail offering around two types of products: made-in-house items that better leverage high-value and high-usage components and b) bought-out-finished or outsourced products that fit the portfolio strategy. Businesses must stop wasting resources and using brute force to design, source, and produce low-value and low-volume items for the residual areas of the matrix. Most companies don't make any money on low-value made in-house SKUs. They don't even know the actual costs of making these items available at the tail since it's harder to account for complexity as we approach the end of the curve. The best way to overcome this issue is to resell someone else's product using a TCO plus formula to calculate the price.

Outsourcing makes pricing low-volume SKUs a simple and straightforward task since the supplier's invoice undoubtedly defines the most significant cost element in the TCO. The finished product becomes the equivalent to your material cost for in-house made items. Ideally, you want to buy from a supplier for whom your twenty product is part of the supplier's eighty product offering. The supplier's core business is producing what you consider to be a low-volume, noncore item, giving you access to new capabilities, external expertise, adding value to your overall marketing strategy. Buying from an outside source allows you to stay focused on what you do best - core products and services.

However, in spite of the value in reducing internal complexity, many organizations still resist outsourcing efforts. One reason is that managers fail to realize the entire cost picture associated with low-volume products, due to the lack of clear separation between the eighty and the twenty items, leading to distortions in the cost data. Managers tend to compare the internal variable cost to the piece price from the supplier, ignoring true product profitability. They often cannot see the hidden cost of complexity associated with the TCO of noncore items, such as indirect and peripheral costs not accurately captured (or misallocated) by traditional absorption cost accounting. A second common reason is an organizational culture fascinated with designing, buying, and manufacturing products in-house — the "not-invented-here" and "not-made-here" attitude.

Beyond high-value products (the eighty), there are

benefits from keeping in-house production of highly profitable low-volume items (the twenty), as long as we can differentiate the manufacturing between core and noncore. Typically, the twenty products we make in-house should have high levels of BOM similarity with the eighty. They often sell to the core, strategic, high-potential customers, and baby-whales. We should also keep in-house items containing sensitive intellectual property.

Concerning the make-versus-buy dilemma, the choice hinges on the business model adopted and on what we are trying to accomplish. When sourcing for the long tail, the decision factors transcend procurement and manufacturing. Product and marketing strategies primarily guide make-versus-buy decisions. Manufacturers should mostly focus on products that help make quadrant one better. However, if you are a distributor, outsourcing is your core business. You will have significantly more vendor activity in quadrant one and should separate your supply chain strategies between quadrants one and three. Distributors also need a more dynamic and frictionless way to source and offer products for the tail.

In general, for non-standard items (non-COTS), you want to look for specialized suppliers or those vendors that focus on product lines that are considered ancillary to you. By partnering with such vendors and tapping into their marketing expertise, you can eventually turn ancillary products into eighty SKUs. There are plenty of expert suppliers making use of third-party distribution channels outside of their core markets. A marginal product line can suddenly become core as companies partner to explore a new brand or region.

Off-the-shelf, commodity items (COTS), having little or no intellectual property associated with, should be outsourced using rules-based procurement, such as reverse auctions or e-auctions. E-auctions are advantageous if correctly applied to low-value twenty products, which you intend to resell. The original goal of reverse auctions was to help buyers procure commodities and other mass-produced goods, and they should not be used to buy bottleneck items or critical services, where price alone is a lesser concern.

As far as conventional procurement is concerned, whether you are buying directly from a supplier or through a reverse auction, you are still carrying some of the logistical and managing costs associated with purchased products. Nevertheless, whenever creating a new commercial ecosystem to expand the long tail, companies have the opportunity to negotiate more favorable terms and conditions with vendors to reduce the burden, using digital platforms such as virtual marketplaces.

A virtual marketplace is an efficient method for direct sourcing and selling third-party products to consumers and businesses. They allow vendors to do business directly with your customers, via your virtual store, under your terms and conditions. Famous examples in business-to-consumer applications are Amazon and eBay while companies like Alibaba, Grainger, ThomasNet, and EWorldTrade play in the business-to-business segment. There are many online marketplaces where manufacturing companies can go to test the concept and get closer to suppliers.

Traditional manufacturing and distribution companies are finding ways to use virtual stores to augment their brick-and-mortar capabilities. Companies like Paccar Parts, for example, a division of global truck manufacturer Paccar, has an online store to sell truck replacement parts. Paccar Parts sells its original brands through Paccar dealers and also sells all-makes parts under a private label called TRP Parts. Most original equipment and aftermarket suppliers to Paccar sell directly via the TRP website to fleets and dealers. Vendors can, in many cases, showcase their products using their brands and SKU references. TRP has a direct shipment program that allows a Paccar dealer or a supplier to send the part directly from their warehouses and plants to the customer.

Virtual marketplaces transfer the costs of doing business in the long tail, such as logistics and warehousing, to the seller. Their role is to sell, take orders, collect payments, and track deliveries of the product from the supplier to the customer, releasing payment to the vendor after deducting a fee. The marketplace owner gets to use data for marketing analytics and receives the benefit of attracting new buyers, based on the availability of low-volume or specialty items. For smaller manufacturers and distributors, selling on third-party virtual marketplaces is a way to give their products greater exposure and tap into a larger audience without having to invest in the web store and marketing to promote the site.

Virtual marketplaces should not yet be considered the ultimate or the only procurement solution in the business. There is still a need to manage strategic supplier contracts and logistics to optimize material cost and TCO for our eighty products. However, virtual marketplaces are evolving fast and improving the supply chain efficiency for low-volume products by reducing the distance between customers and suppliers. As far as supplying finished products to create a powerful long tail, they are both sourcing and marketing tools at the same time.

Producing a wide variety of SKUs in-house

In any business, there are different options to make products and services available to customers. The two most basic ways are buying from vendors and producing in-house. Whichever ways we use to build the offering, there will always be a mix of high and low-volume products to be delivered to both eighty and twenty customers. One dilemma for the company is how to meet the demands of eighty clients for customized products, without incurring extra costs and destroying profitability. Another difficulty is how to supply a large variety of twenty SKUs efficiently to a myriad of large and small customers.

Companies want to be able to produce custom-tailored and low-volume products near mass production costs. This objective is precisely the goal of mass customization in manufacturing or "the capability to manufacture a relatively high volume of product options for a relatively large market (or collection of niche markets) that demands customization, without tradeoffs in cost, delivery, and quality."[xix] Mass customization is an essential concept for masters of complexity and is associated with leading-edge production technologies like additive manufacturing.

However, before we adopt the new approaches and technologies, we should better understand the prerequisites for mass customization, in terms of process and product configurations. Process-wise, we need to have complete separation between eighty and twenty, to increase supply chain agility and keep the focus on high-value areas. On the product side, some level of modularity is necessary, in line with the standardization efforts discussed, such as design-for-manufacturing-and-assembly principles (DFMA). These are overarching principles that must be followed to accommodate the variety in mass production.

The physical separation between eighty and twenty is a Lean principle. We must have a free-of-interferences, smooth, customer-focused process to achieve Lean. We accomplish that by placing an ultra-high focus on a select group of customers and products (the eighty), to avoid distractions. The production of the eighty should happen in different lines, buildings, or business units, under a completely different supply chain model. The separation keeps the complexity created by the twenty products isolated from the eighty.

We ground the process around highly-efficient, automated, single-piece-flow production lines called in-lines. An in-line is a dedicated group of machines and raw materials laid out in sequence, producing a single product or a very similar family of products, building a single unit at a time, while continuously performing all of the operations required to meet the demands of the customer in a timely fashion. There is no need to change the in-line setup when there is a change in the product specification. In-lines organize the work on the shop floor by value stream and not by function.

For greater supply chain agility, we uncouple the

demand side from the supply side of an in-line. We use pull-systems like kanbans to feed the materials from suppliers, and MRD (market rate of demand) to drive production flow and rhythm. To use a definition from ITW (Illinois Tool Works), "MRD is a replenishment scheduling system based upon producing or replenishing products at the rate of demand. Demand means the actual consumption of products rather than forecasted consumption. If used correctly, MRD helps business units to achieve high levels of customer service while helping to prevent inventory buildup and inventory shortages. The MRD approach to inventory replenishment and production scheduling is more effective than the traditional 'push' methods. Market demand dictates how many parts should be produced; therefore, materials are 'pulled' into production based on consumption."[xx]

There is no sales forecasting involved when planning for the making of the eighty. The market and customer control the drumbeat. There are buffers of materials and products on both ends to account for delivery times and fluctuations, but there is no accounting penalty for stopping the line, such as lack of absorption, once the customer buffer is full. There are also no indirect or estimated costs allocated to eighty products. You get to work with the real product cost and contribution margin. In conventional accounting, the indirect production overhead, like quality inspectors, for example, is distributed amongst the products. In-lines use direct costing, meaning that only costs that vary with the production affect the contribution margin. All the indirect overhead incurred during the month goes into the P&L as a separate line called period costs. The separate period cost line allows managers to deal with issues promptly and keeps accounting from polluting the margin of high-value products.

Once we know the direct costs for the eighty, it's easier to understand the real costs for the twenty by subtracting the eighty from the total. Low-volume and high-variety factories can use conventional manufacturing as long as the product portfolio has been streamlined and reduced. The typical production occurs in batches, driven by the sales forecast. To account for inaccuracies, companies allow themselves longer lead-times and carry a little inventory of these products. The two-factory approach provides for a continuous focus on lowering costs, improving quality, and reducing delivery times for the eighty SKUs while streamlining the twenty and charging accordingly for true profitability.

Along with the separation between high and low-value, we must also consider the product configuration since the more we design products based on DFMA and modularity, the more effective mass customization becomes. We want to be able to use basic modules and products to produce a large number of variants, instead of having to use sub-assemblies or other modifications to create new ones. We also want to design products in a way that we can postpone the variety and the customization until the end of the assembly process.

Waiting until the end of the line to finish a low-volume or highly customized product, is a way to increase true profitability at the tail. This technique, commonly referred to as postponement, is a form of late-stage completion as close to demand as possible. For instance, Cummins has some very efficient in-lines to produce different base engine platforms without much human interventions and setups. Once the in-line assembles a base engine, it sends it to different finishing lines, based on the levels of customization required. At the finishing line (could be a twenty line), the engines receive unique parts and control software, according to each specific application (marine, oil-and-gas, generator-set, and automotive for example).

Depending on the types of options specified, Cummins has the opportunity to finish the product in-house or to involve a distributor that is closest to the customer to add some unique parts and assemblies, which can be mounted on the product or delivered as a kit. For example, the distributor in Houston may add some very different oil-and-gas accessories, which are not typically available at the Cummins factory. Postponement allows the business to capture the profits from the eighty in-line while making variety available to customers and minimizing inventory and errors for everyone. The modularity of the engine design coupled with the product specification language, and the agility of the supply chain, help maintain an attractive portfolio for Cummins.

Once product and process configurations are optimized, companies need to decide what types of customization they will offer and how they are going to deliver it. As per the article on HBR, "The Four Faces of Mass Customization,"[xxi] four different approaches are identified. The first one is "collaborative customization" where the company joins forces with the customer to select the unique features, based on a product specification language, such as the one Cummins uses to select engine options. Many companies make product configurators available online that help specify the product features and options for a given customer. For instance, Zenni Optical, the online eyewear retailer, offers a way for customers to perform 3D trials using the video camera on their computers. The optical frames can just as quickly be produced on-demand using a 3D printer in the future.

The second form is known as "adaptive customization" or the inherent characteristic of a product to adapt or customize itself for specific customer demand and usage situations. Adaptive customization is rapidly growing due to the extensive usage of connected devices and artificial intelligence (AI). Machine learning, a subset of AI, is the ability that a machine has to perform a task without explicit instructions, based on patterns and data gained from input devices like sensors. More and more mechanical products are incorporating electronic controls that grant adaptive capabilities. From coffee makers to airplanes, these devices learn from a customers' unique requirements and job duty-cycles to change their operating modes and customize on the fly.

The self-propelled vacuum cleaner from iRobot, named Roomba, is an excellent example of adaptive customization that has been around for a while. The small machine learns over time how to adjust and optimize the cleaning routines by picking the best routes and mapping the rooms in the house. The bot is also capable of recharging and discharging the accumulated dirt by itself, and can also determine the cleaning cycles based on the room size.

"Cosmetic customization" is the third approach to personalize products based on colors, logos, packaging, and other identifiers that provide a unique presentation. Although there may be less value-added in cosmetic tailoring, there is still significant and growing value from the customer's point of view. From personalized medicine, clothing, footwear, TV commercials, and beverages, numerous hard benefits come from cosmetic customization, ranging from price premiums to increased customer loyalty. High-speed technologies are available to customize products during in-line production, such as three-axis hybrid laser markers that engrave onto all types of materials, for tracking and personalization.

The fourth approach is known as "transparent customization," when the business provides custom products and services based solely on their market knowledge, analytics capability, or because customer needs are predictable or easily deduced. Different customers get to buy different products without the knowledge that they are buying customized services or products. This method is growing thanks to the abundance of data related to customer's preferences and buying patterns. Financial institutions and advertising services, such as AdWords and AdSense from Google use transparent customization to adapt their services to unique customer preferences.

As you can infer from the examples above, mass customization is not exclusive to manufacturing companies. Distribution and service businesses have multiple ways to deliver tailored products at large-scale production costs just as well. Auto parts wholesalers and distributors, for example, have been assembling custom repair kits for the do-it-yourself end-users and mechanics for many years. Wholesalers also know the importance of separating high and low-value inventories in their warehouses. They keep distinct areas for each and hardly put-away the fast-moving parts, using cross-docking operations and direct shipment from suppliers to keep up with production. Separation and modularity are enablers to profitable mass customization for all types of companies.

Very few companies have a business model that is almost entirely reliant on the long tail. Companies like Amazon and Alibaba are virtually exceptions because of their singularities, timing to market, scale, and intense focus on internet distribution and online retail. Regardless of size and type of business, when we combine the data on customers and products under 80/20, we realize that every company has a long tail. We may not recognize its effect on the overall profitability, but the tail is never neutral. Still, not every company has a strategy to keep the long tail lucrative and to make it work for them.

We know the long tail can be helpful if built using a low complexity model grounded on true profitability. However, it can just as well be detrimental if we let too many freeloaders and low-value SKUs and customers to enter. It can easily damage the bottom-line by robbing the gains from the head of the demand curve. The solution lies in the ability to maintain the tail's agility and profitability, paying constant attention to sales turnover patterns. You want to minimize freeloaders, but you also want to lessen the number of dormant products and inactive customers in the tail.

Let's not forget that the primary goal is to make the core business more substantial and more profitable, using the long tail as a source for future eighty and transitional buyers. We also want the long tail to be a cradle for blockbuster products and the best reservoir to develop high-value customers. Most eighty customers start small, buying low-value SKUs at first. They stay with the firm and buy more because they receive good value for their money. As every marketer knows, it's a lot less costly to develop an existing twenty customer into an eighty, than convincing a new eighty customer to leave a competitor and start buying from you.

A well managed long tail can be a formidable generator of new customers, a laboratory for innovative products, a marketplace for vendor partnerships, and the best source to gather customer data. We use it to mine for new core buyers, create awareness and preference for products or services, and increase loyalty to keep them buying. The data from the tail is vital to know why and how customers buy, to identify which customers to focus on, and to find more. We always discover segments, regions, channels, and other groupings that are dormant or underrepresented in the analysis.

However, the list of potential buyers can be incredibly vast and fragmented, and you can't possibly reach every possibility without spending incredible amounts of money. Analytics is essential to select targets with greater precision and granularity. It's also the best way to find and attract buyers when we use the data to carry on cluster analysis, to discover groups of similar customers based on analytical modeling. The simplest and most straightforward way to perform cluster analysis is to use 80/20 to model the data. By doing so, we can compare various market segments and decide which targets to prioritize and how to approach them.

Companies already have a wealth of transactional data that they can use. However, it needs to be captured and enhanced with the desired segmentation criteria that are most useful for the analysis. To improve the data is to add dimensions that are typically indifferent, or unknown to customers and yet helpful to the company when performing cluster analysis. Companies use demographic (business-to-consumer) or firmographics (business-to-business) criteria to segment customers. Demographics are the easiest to apply since based on physical and palpable characteristics: for example, the industry which the customer belongs to, the customer location and company size in terms of turnover.

We can also use needs-based segmentation, which is a more sophisticated approach that accounts for buying decision factors that drive customer behavior, for example, low prices, high levels of customer service, company reputation, quality, technology level, ease of doing business and product usage intensity. Behavioral segmentation has to do with how customers act when buying from a supplier. These are similar to personal characteristics, many times enforced by buyers within the organization. Loyalty (relationship level), risk-taking (early or late adopter), urgency (planning practices), and time horizon (long term agreements) to mention a few.

Segmenting the business by relevant criteria is the surest way to converge on the high-value and growing portions of the market. 80/20 cluster analytics allows you to objectively quantify and compare different segments currently buried in the original customer and product matrix. It re-cuts the first dataset into a few new ones, comparing their quad analyses against the original and versus each other.

6.3 Segment Cluster Analysis

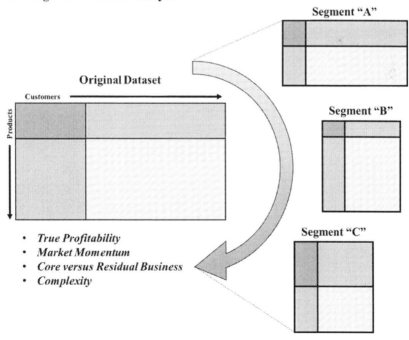

The first aspect to look at is true profitability by segment and by quad within each cluster. A higher TrP margin points to a more exceptional ability to be perceived by the market as delivering superior value. It also shows efficiency from a resource utilization standpoint. The company can create more value with less overhead. The opposite is also helpful to know. There could be market segments where the company is not set up to make any money.

The second criterion is the growth potential. In most cases, companies should be able to recognize right away if they have room to expand, based on market expertise and research. They can also ascertain growth momentum in the segment, by comparing the eighty business with market research data from internal or external sources, such as government, industry organizations, and primary research companies. Another question is the company's growth rate compared to the overall market.

We must also compare the proportions of the matrices to understand the amounts of core versus low-value and the residual business, for example. How deep or how complex is the product offering in quad three and how broad or transaction-intensive is the customer base in quad two. The density of the data in each matrix gives us an idea about the general level of activity. By examing the similarity indices and supply chains for each customer grouping, we have a better idea of the internal complexity created by each segment.

Cluster analysis results in a more objective evaluation of each target segment. Masters of complexity use analytical models, usually based on Pareto, to sweep the customer data for new patterns continuously. The algorithms are always spotting niches and groupings underrepresented in the current portfolio by concurrently analyzing and comparing large numbers of subsets, with impressive acuity and speed. This process allows companies to collect different distributions or super-Paretos, which are extremely valuable when designing marketing strategies.

For an attractive cluster they want to pursue, they use the demographics for more precise and targeted ways to address a broader audience. For example, they seek out the target populations using influencers to propel certain product lines. A small amount of marketing dollars goes a long way to create a positive brand image and preference for your products if the target population is already predisposed to buy a specific type of item versus the general population.

The evolution of shopping analytics, virtual marketplaces, and the ability to mass customize products and services are only a few methods companies have to excel at marketing the long tail. The pure e-tailers such as Amazon combine digital tools with highly-efficient distribution and logistics, using centralized warehouses and reducing the number of physical locations. The web and mobile storefronts are incredibly suited to showcasing all the SKUs available in the long tail.

Brick-and-mortar retailers and manufacturers are realizing that to attract new buyers and collect data for customer analytics, they need to adopt a hybrid model known by the jargon "brick-and-click," by which a company integrates both offline and online presences. They need to integrate all the ways by which customers transact with the company, including conventional means used by manufacturers, such as phone, catalogs, and face-to-face.

We can find multiple examples of brick-and-click companies in different industries, such as health care, car sales, home furnishings, appliances, apparel, department store, food, and groceries. However, conventional manufacturing is also waking up to this transactional approach, where the brick-and-mortar infrastructure is a natural extension of the online presence. Truck manufacturer Scania, for example, offer ways for customers to start the purchasing journey online, configuring the truck for different types of jobs or applications, and finish with its delivery at the nearby Scania dealer. Users have a configurator portal[xxii] online which includes a vast number of options related to Scania's modular product architecture.

Shopping data and patterns are so relevant that

companies must find ways to convince customers to transact online. Having an institutional and informative website is no longer enough. Transactional data is a seed that can develop into a robust analytical database when we augment primary data with demographics and unstructured information captured from the internet. The long tail allows companies to attract customers to transact online, or at least to start the process and finish the purchase at the store or in person.

Governing Complexity

The paradox is that simplicity leads to complexity, and vice-versa, and both can be good or bad at the same time. Indeed, complexity can be both detrimental and beneficial in business, depending on how we use and control it. It's also true that this paradox only exists in the mind of those who don't have a clear definition of complexity. Thus, because most managers can't define or measure it for the organization, they have a hard time recognizing and attacking the problem.

Truthfully, the closer we are to the problem, the less perspective and definition we have. We get too involved in the detailed work and lose sight of the big picture. The problem with excessive part count and duplication, for example, is not immediately evident or relevant for an engineer designing a new product. It's not that he or she doesn't care, but they are too close and too involved in the design work. However, the issue does become apparent when we take a step back and realize that, at the product line or business unit level, the BOM similarity is too low and we have too much overhead and too many suppliers. The farthest removed you are from the trenches, the easier it is to recognize complexity.

In most organizations, complexity is everyone's problem and no one's responsibility. Another paradox! Especially true for those that do not leverage the long tail to their advantage. Nevertheless, managers are responsible for defining complexity to the organization in terms of metrics (what), responsibilities (who) and processes (how). It must be actively governed, either to help the business (as in the long tail) or to keep it from hurting profitability (as in excessive freeloaders).

The purpose of governance is to maximize true profitability by controlling complexity. It accomplishes that by optimizing the portfolio, regulating what enters and what leaves the offering, sponsoring product design methods that foster standardization and modularity, and maintaining a healthy pipeline of profit-improvement projects. Successful governance does not need additional resources or overhead to take place. The key is to embed the new ways of working within the functions and processes that create complexity in the first place. We are referring to areas like engineering, procurement, and sales as well as cross-functional teams like new product introduction (NPI), product planning and management (PPM) and improvement project pipelines.

6.4 Complexity Governance is Central

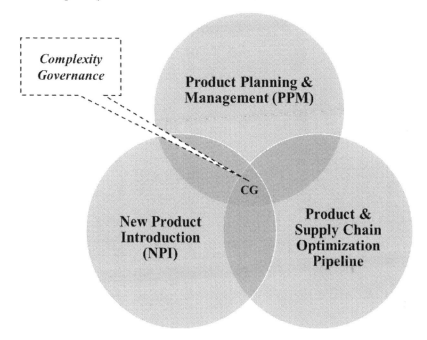

At the same time, we need metrics and KPIs that are intrinsically connected to the success of the business, to keep governance from becoming a mere administrative exercise, with no teeth. That should not be a problem if we accept that the ultimate metric is true profitability, which in aggregate, leads to the company's overall operating profit. We're not just watching over every line in the income statement, but we're managing every product and customer P&L that forms the EBIT line. Here's an example of how the metrics work together.

6.5 Complexity KPIs Embedded in Processes

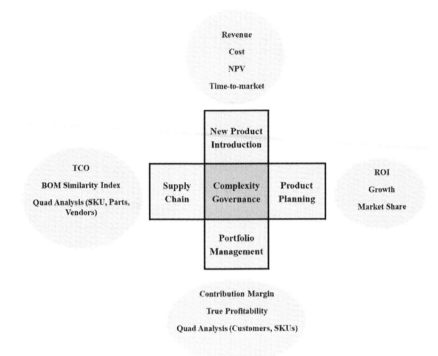

Complexity governance requires four essential components to be effective. First is the leadership presence to define complexity for the organization and articulate how it becomes an integral part of its success or failure. Masters of complexity have a clear vision of how to use it to win in the market. It's part of their business model and permeates from the top to all levels in the organization. Successful simplifiers also have clear goals and objectives to tackle complexity in its various forms. On top of senior executive engagement, companies need to designate a chief complexity officer or manager to coordinate the entire process, ensuring that true profitability goals are met. They also need skilled people within each function to lead the adoption of new methods and ways of working.

The second ingredient is a decision-making forum or cross-functional structure to serve as a governing body to the overall complexity management process. Most companies use existing cross-functional teams, such as new product introduction (NPI) and product planning and management (PPM) to incorporate the role of complexity governance. If these are well-managed and well-connected processes in the company, the PPM can be an excellent forum to receive the expanded mandate (product planning and complexity management). For instance, PPCM would create and instill a design-for-variety method to R&D and become the final decision maker during NPI gate reviews and also when it comes to profit improvement projects in the pipeline.

Third, we need new methods and ways of working within each function and process. Emphasis should be given for the adoption of tools and techniques discussed before, to achieve standardization and smart variety. We change work habits, and routines through a combination of performance management, incentives, training, talent replacement and the selection of complexity-minded operating platforms, such as engineering design software that takes reuse and switchability into account.

Lastly, we need data analytics and new KPIs to

monitor progress towards simplification and to condition the long tail. Model-based analytics is essential to businesses that want to offer variety and higher levels of customization as a means to attract customers. The ability to model demand and manage complexity with Pareto is critical to understand the value of diversification and customization. For instance, using quadrant analysis to monitor progress is helpful because, aside from being data-driven, it allows the company to visualize each source of complexity independently. A structured, model-based analytical tool is invaluable to govern complexity. Next, we will discuss how masters of complexity use Pareto-based analytics to boost true profitability.

7 PARETO ANALYTICS

We can't even begin to imagine the amount of data collected on individuals and businesses. Whether you are a click-only or brick-and-click company, there are data tracks everywhere telling who you are, what you do, and all other aspects of your existence. While you may have confidential information and trade secrets locked-up somewhere, your overt activities are being recorded, shared, and analyzed continuously by someone at this very moment. The "big data" containing both organized and unorganized records are used to reveal patterns, trends, and associations.

Although data has become a cheap commodity, the expertise to extract valuable insight from the analysis is more precious and indispensable than ever. It's like the know-how to transform a bunch of sand into a powerful microprocessor. The ability is prized, because there are countless hurdles involved in converting raw bits into actionable insight, including the selection of proper sources and pieces. Using low-quality or ignoring a critical part of the data can completely change the outcome and lead to wrong decisions.

The power and usefulness of business analytics helped propel an industry built on retrieving, organizing, visualizing, and extracting meaning from big data. Firms offer custom and off-the-shelf solutions that can elevate the analysis from merely descriptive reporting to fully predictive and prescriptive decision tools, augmented by artificial intelligence (AI) and machine learning (ML). Nevertheless, business analytics is nothing new. Since its beginning, general accounting used different forms of analytics to produce actionable insights. Electronic spreadsheets, such as Microsoft Excel, have been around for almost forty years now, and have contributed significantly to the propagation of analytics in decision making. Managers are getting used to more prescriptive and data-rich forms of analysis that can often be counterintuitive.

In the last two decades, we saw new solutions emerge, including business intelligence (BI) applications, which take electronic spreadsheets to an entirely new level. Tableau, for example, has grown to become one of the most popular BI tools in the world. It allows non-technical users to visualize their data in a better and faster way, helping generate decision-making insights. One of the significant advantages of modern BI tools is the fact that, differently from electronic spreadsheets, they can quickly and automatically connect with databases to extract and synchronize information, allowing for real-time visualization.

Excel and Tableau are very compelling instruments; however, they are not sufficient to give managers all they need, including the critical insight and wisdom to make the right choices. Without decision frameworks to select and interpret the data, they fail to predict or to prescribe actions. When we use Tableau, for example, our ability to make correlations and understand what has happened is enhanced, but if we do not apply our intelligence and experience to build upon the data, we are not in a position to best judge what to do next. Still, managers sometimes behave as if, merely knowing how to use BI gives them the automatic ability to predict the future and make insightful decisions. They reinforce a management paradigm from the days when data was hard to come by. A belief that whoever owns the data has the last word. Data always trumped opinions, no matter the source or the presentation format. We used to hear managers joke, "In God we trust, and everyone else brings data." Nowadays, having only data doesn't mean much.

There can also be a dark side to analytics, where managers may be inclined to pick and choose only data that best aligns with their views and package it nicely using visualization tools. A well-meaning manager with an agenda, equipped with Tableau and loaded with selective data, can be a powerful weapon to influence decisions. When making choices using pure BI, managers are implicitly adopting mental models and applying wisdom to make the calls. Unfortunately, even data-based decisions can be influenced by judgment biases and blind spots, but it doesn't mean we shouldn't use BI to make choices. Quite the contrary. When we apply a proven framework on top of Excel or Tableau, such as a statistical model, our predictive and prescriptive capabilities are greatly enhanced.

Companies need a combination of people-based and model-based analytics. The bigger the data, the higher the need for model-based analytics, which uses experiential and verifiable algorithms to shape the analysis and to capture and communicate the results. Achieving excellent results is a combination of knowledge and experience, joined with proven operating models or "guardrails" to stay away from collective delusion and disasters. It's like saying, "In God we trust, and everyone else brings insight based on a proven model."

A high degree of confusion remains between what a BI tool delivers and the data work required to make BI useful. Proper data preparation is an absolute necessity in moving from a basic BI capability into BI excellence. The data ingredients do not by themselves, make the soufflé but require data preparation, transformation, and enrichment, combined with the metrics, KPIs, and dimensions needed. The BI solution is not then merely the software application but must include a data transformation roadmap to support the various required insights across the organizations. For every decision in marketing, sales, finance, and operations, for example, there is an optimized data pool that can give valuable and critical insights, explored via the BI tool. The approach is to design an analytics data pool that is relevant to its users versus a data lake where the users "drown" in data overload.

The other confusion is how to make the BI tool and associated reports relevant and insightful. Does it answer the "so what" question and what next step actions can be drawn? Many times BI reports seem to increase without reason and in effect, create confusions and complexity in bringing real value to the business. KPI reports are often not enough as there needs to be a context or a causal explanation – why did we underperform, what are the drivers, can we rectify them, how?

A step up from traditional BI is model-based analytics. Here the use of rules, algorithms, and models are developed to perform predictive and simulated analytics. What happens to our business performance if x, y, z occurs. These analytical models are looking to move beyond the Excel domain into a more dynamic, robust, and automatable modeling process that benefits the many. Analytical models can touch all aspects of a business (finance, sales, marketing, supply chain, operations), as long as the digitalization process has occurred. Even equipment and assets can benefit from analytical models. In the world of IoT (Internet of Things), the discussion today is about predictive maintenance, quality control, and optimized asset performance. The impact of the data scientist revolution is leading to a re-evaluation as to where analytical modeling, machine learning, and AI can create new dynamic routines to optimize processes and create efficiencies.

Some companies need to automate specific administrative routines to speed-up decisions, but there is always an element of collaboration between people and processes. For instance, larger retailers use model-based analytics to adjust SKU prices and simulate the outcome of different pricing strategies. These models are created based on customer buying patterns, observed and analyzed via artificial intelligence. Kroger, the grocery store chain, uses the data on competitors, promotions, and sales from its stores and from outside to optimize prices. Model-based analytics helps managers adapt and change prices and promotions immediately based on buyer insights.

Another example is Kohl's, the department store retail chain. They go beyond predicting the impact of pricing strategies to help managers make decisions. The system called Actionable Analytics serves weekly tasks and recommendations via the associate's dashboard to improve results. Kohl's uses model-based analytics to prescribe store managers action items to better drive sales in their stores.

At the foundation of all these mission-critical processes, we find proven analysis models or frameworks. For example, a system that predicts equipment life will use a lot of sensor data and inputs, like vibration, and temperature to feed the model. We can always visualize these data points using spreadsheets and BI dashboards. However, when it comes time to predicting the end of life of an expensive machine and deciding whether to invest the replacement capital, the system relies on a statistical model known as Weibull Distribution. Widely used in reliability and life data analysis, Weibull provides the necessary foundation and guardrails for decision-making. At a minimum, the model helps us organize and interpret the data in a more efficient way.

Many models are based on statistical criteria, like Weibull, while others use machine learning and observation, with a lot of fine-tuning and calibration. Businesses have long discovered the power of Pareto as an experiential framework to train algorithms and to manage true profitability. What we call 80/20 analytics is a simpler and faster way to discover imbalances and to separate high and low-value elements using big data.

Before going any further, and at the risk of explaining what is already understood, it may be helpful to remind ourselves about the Pareto Principle briefly.

Vital few and trivial many

Over the years, Pareto's Principle, otherwise known as the 80/20 Rule, has been used in multiple ways to enhance business performance. In 1941, the quality consultant Joseph Juran named this empirical principle after its Italian proposer Vilfredo Pareto. In this simple rule, Juran recognized a powerful business tool that helped ignite the quality revolution in Japan during the mid-1950s. The principle is known by a few other names, including the law of the vital few and the trivial many, the principle of imbalance, and the principle of factor sparsity.

The 80/20 rule states that, for many events, roughly eighty percent of the effects come from twenty percent of the causes. We can observe such an imbalance across many areas in life and business. Eighty percent of revenue comes from twenty percent of the customers. Eighty percent of profits come from twenty percent of the products. Eighty percent of sales generated by twenty percent of the salespeople. Eighty percent of material purchases come from twenty percent of suppliers.

Disparities are everywhere.

In almost every situation, there is significant inequality between causes and effects. The amount of effort does not correlate with the sum of results. However, it doesn't mean that you will always get an exact 80:20 ratio. 80/20 is not a precise distribution pattern, but a pointer to a proportion that is continually occurring in nature. You can have a situation where 95% of the results come from 12% of the efforts, or where 78% of the outcomes derive from 3% of the causes. It's very unusual to find a situation where results and efforts turn out to be approximately the same.

This observation implies that not all things are equal and that some inputs can generate far higher outputs than others. It is also consistent with the accepted notion that people, decisions, products, and customers are not all the same. Some have more firepower than others. To paraphrase the familiar marketing maxim, "some customers are a lot more equal than others."

From time management and resource allocation perspectives, it means one of two things: either that we spend time on initiatives that matter, or that we waste time on activities that do not make much difference in the scheme of things. Spreading your attention evenly, across the total number of inputs, is not the optimal way to achieve the best results. If you work on the vital few things that matter most, you will tip the scale of the natural imbalance in your favor. By isolating the critical few from the trivial many and by increasing your focus on the twenty percent that creates eighty percent of the value, you will boost your outcomes significantly. Ignoring the imbalance and focusing on the trivial many will not only diminish your results but also destroy any business over time.

Key Pareto Indicators (KPIs)

Smart, analytical companies, resort to the age-proven Pareto Principle to extract actionable insights from big data. The inexorability of imbalances in the numbers and the necessity to clearly distinguish between low and high-value elements are forcing algorithms to learn and to incorporate this familiar model. No matter the size of the portfolio, 80/20 analytics keeps pointing to the fact that only a handful of customers and products create the majority of margin dollars and growth, for example. The number of 80/20 adepts grows with the expansion of big data, using AI and ML to condition the models. Similar to teaching algorithms to recognize pictures, we train them to recognize Pareto patterns, as per Michael Schrage's article naming three different approaches to training: Smart Paretos, Super-Pareto's, and Supra Paretos. These are consistent with the way masters of complexity use big data analytics to govern the long tail.

The first approach, Smart Paretos, instills 80/20-like distributions into everyday models, allowing companies to quickly and automatically identify and separate the eighty (vital few) from the twenty (trivial many). Every dataset goes through a Pareto's filter to uncover imbalances in customer purchases, product sales, part number usage, supplier concentration, and every other dataset that enters the model. The screening saves time and energy, releasing managers to focus on results rather than conditioning data. Extracting, cleaning, and organizing information consumes the majority of time and resources.

Direct correlations between associated datasets are made to uncover patterns and new ideas. We can, for example, use Smart Paretos to single out the customers that buy more, buy more frequently and with better margins, to offer exclusive incentives and promotions. We can also instruct the algorithms to identify mix issues within core customers, so we can try to influence the list of products they buy. Every company should make their analytics smarter by training the models to recognize imbalances.

The second approach, or Super-Pareto's, helps companies identify unique patterns of imbalance in the data, other than usual 80/20-like ratios. Super-Pareto's are outlier distributions like 55/1 and 45/70 ratios, for instance, that keep showing up in segments of the data. It's essential to know them since they usually contain a pattern that we want to either replicate or avoid. A ratio of 55/1 is a super-sparse-Pareto, which means that only a few factors are driving the vast majority of the results. Schrage mentions a typical example in his HBR article, where "less than 0.25% of mobile gamers are responsible for half of all in-game revenue."[xxiii]

An example on the other extreme would be a super-tail-Pareto such as 45/70, where it takes seventy percent of the inputs to create forty-five percent of the results. Think of an online retailer that focuses on selling low-volume items instead of a usual mix between high and low-volume. This e-tailer could be trying to use the long tail alone as a business model. It takes many SKUs and a lot of sales activity to generate only a fraction of the revenues. This ratio can denote an ineffectual retailing and distribution model since the company needs a considerable effort to accomplish only mediocre results. Companies train algorithms to raise flags whenever they spot outlier distributions happening frequently.

Super-Pareto's are everywhere in business, and it typically takes a while before they are recognized and validated. Pareto-based analytics provides faster recognition across different datasets, allowing managers to identify multiple ratios and use them with confidence when making decisions. Based on the mobile gamers example above, managers should decide to use marketing money differently between the recurring 0.25% that drive most of the sales versus all other users. The small fraction of super users are the influencers or the ones you want to stay close to, for instance, giving exclusive access to product launches and events.

The collection of different ratios leads to Supra-Pareto's or combinations of KPIs, defined here as Key Pareto Indicators, from interrelated datasets. The KPIs are used to drive up true profitability and govern complexity. For product managers and marketing, for example, there is particular interest in correlating product and customer KPIs. Engineering and purchasing will want to combine data from products, components, and suppliers. The KPI related to purchases from core customers, which drives certain combinations of parts and suppliers, are extremely valuable to foster BOM similarity and vendor rationalization.

Online retailers use Supra-Pareto's to recognize and classify the marketing dynamics of certain product lines. They identify the many long tails associated with the portfolio and their true profitability. They also detect the super users or eighty buyers for each product or service category. These super users can be addressed separately from everyone else, from a communications standpoint. The simplicity and straightforwardness of Pareto-based-analytics make it easier to create better insights and strategies faster. 80/20 analytics enables masters of complexity to work comfortably in the long tail. They correlate and integrate structured and unstructured data to predict and prescribe, achieving a better trade-off between variety and scalability.

Translating Super-Paretos into business reality

To better illustrate the application benefits, let us imagine that our data scientists have now deployed our Super-Pareto analytics engine. The engine can automatically discover the multitude of Pareto relationships that exist in every data direction of XYZ Corporation. This capability gives every business function the ability to identify and explore these Pareto relationships. However, equally important, the business has been trained to explore these relationships with questions regarding growth opportunities, resources, investments, and marketing. Perhaps the 80/20 distribution is valid for the company overall, but for a highly profitable sub-category and channel, it's more like 98/2 since only a few sales reps can effectively pitch a complicated technical sale. For sales, the critical question may be to evaluate the impact of adding one extra sales engineer. We would expect that the ROI should be high and worth an above-average investment in this person salary.

These Pareto evaluations become a springboard of different strategies and activities that the business can practically embrace. They are also significantly more specific, detailed, and realistic compared to the more general and overly optimistic 'hockey stick' business plan seen in many situations. Without a Pareto focus, the business will dilute its effort into the numerous complexity traps that exist in any organization by default. Continuous effort is needed to avoid the natural gravity pull from complexity. By steering the business along with its super Pareto priorities, there is a value alignment that will accelerate and engender positive change both in performance results but also in softer measures such as moral, employee empowerment and client respect.

In our imaginary XYZ Corporation, every function and role is using Pareto analytics to track performance, develop strategies, and define key action steps, resulting in a supercharged business. Top-down edicts become replaced by a multi-level agenda of aligned priorities. These cascading Pareto priorities can support a more proactive and decentralized engagement process by the company. The result is a quicker and more agile business model that can react adequately to the increasingly fast pace and changing market conditions.

What are the elements that need to come together to deliver on a Super Pareto capability? Let's take a case study of a manufacturing business that is looking to use Pareto analysis and true profitability to define its strategic focus and complexity management execution. Model-based analytics needs to be available on-demand with up to date information that supports actionable business-specific insights.

As mentioned, different than spreadsheet exercises, model-based analytics solutions transform what is otherwise an ad-hoc and often manual exercise into a robust platform used for a variety of insights across many areas in an organization. Technically, there are four stages involved in model-based analytics to have a consistent, practical, and effective solution: 1) Data connectivity and quality assurance processes; 2) Multi-data source integration and transformation; 3) Model development and configuration (Pareto); 4) Key insight visualization delivery.

The first and essential stage requires that we source the data in a way that it can be updated automatically, from a reliable and accurate source. The recurrent need to sanitize data issues is not always apparent, but it's crucial to have a source of truth for any analysis. Additionally, the required data is usually not unique but multi-sourced, needing several transformations to supply the model with its inputs. Bringing together financial, ERP, and CRM data into a coherent data structure is not always easy. It needs a dose of planning and data science to identify how best to map apples, oranges, and pears. The work involves data expertise and an understanding of the business context. Each business is unique and therefore requires a process and methodology to avoid getting stuck in detail.

Constructing the model is the critical part but often made more complicated or impossible if the first two stages have not been well designed and executed. Model-based analytics implies that the system or application can systematically run live updates, allowing the engine to perform various calculations using your data. Different levels of sophistication may apply to the model, using multiple frameworks and rules. These can be conditional rules and equational scripts, statistical analyses, or then more complex models using machine learning or artificial intelligence. Finally, the model may embed several calculation layers, a multi-layered construct (like an onion), which follow a sequence before the final result can be processed and delivered.

However, even after having completed the main requirements for model-based analytics, this will be useless unless the insights are relevant and actionable for the key users and stakeholders. The tip of the iceberg, i.e., the real ideas, is where you need to make visible the issues you wish your team to explore, investigate, and take action. As mentioned above, often this is more than merely a dashboard report but a way of displaying information to make clear the what, where, and why of issues requiring attention.

As an example, using the 80/20 analytics model discussed above, how can the results be visualized? The standard dashboard BI tool will not be the best way of exploring and investigating key issues and insights.

Firstly taking on the 80/20 methodology, there needs to be a clear visualization of quadrant results, revenue, and complexity cost.

7.1 Visualizing Value with 80/20 Matrix

Revenue

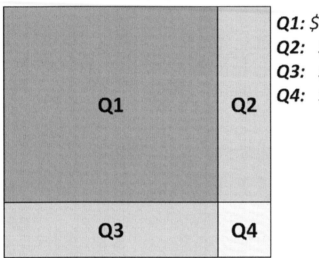

Q1: $32m (64%)
Q2: $8m (16%)
Q3: $8m (16%)
Q4: $2m (4%)

The graphic above gives a clear display of the revenue distribution of our 80/20 model. Q1 represents the juncture where the top 80% of Customer Revenue overlap with 80% of Product Revenue. It is critical that these customers and products are well taken care of and that the business understands the real contribution that this quadrant offers. Importantly, even if Q4 is small in revenues, this quadrant provides a real opportunity to reduce complexity as the chart below highlights.

7.2. The Complexity Picture

Cost of Complexity

Q1	**Q2**	**Q1:** 1.9%
		Q2: 9.8%
Q3	**Q4**	**Q3:** 40.3%
		Q4: 48.1%

By looking at the cost of complexity chart, we have a good indication about which products and customers carry the most overhead. We can start creating separation between the best and the worst areas of the business. Each company's picture will differ from this example but be primarily aligned with the magnitude, creating the opportunity to redirect focus where it brings the highest reward. In effect, this chart visually helps delineate strategies to deal with each of the quadrants. The idea is not merely to scrutinize Q4 from a cost perspective but also look at a multitude of considerations. For example, how does the customer/product portfolio or market segmentation overlay with this quadrant and determine if these are upcoming segments that may soon become Q1? Alternatively, perhaps new processes and service offerings need to change in Q4, e.g., manufacture to order.

The following chart is a more granular representation of the previous one but where the user can then dive into a specific area to find more detail.

7.3 A Typical "Drill-Down" 80/20 Matrix

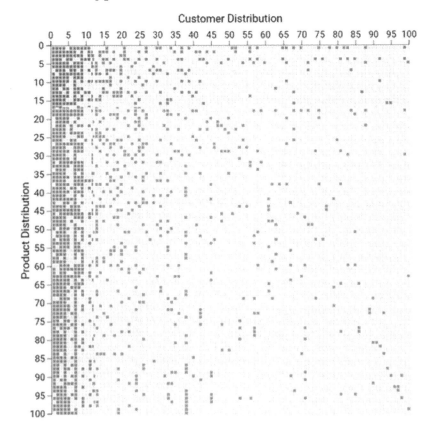

What is graphically compelling is looking at Q4 and observing the true sparsity of customer and product combinations in this area, visually highlighting the hidden space that creates complexity. For each of these areas, explorative analysis can be done to investigate specific actions.

Taking account of these complexity costs allows the model to re-calibrate our understanding as to where profitability occurs. This true profitability picture is typically very different than the company's P&L view, and standard management account reports. A typical complexity cost re-allocation exercise may then lead to a waterfall bridge chart showing the following:

7.4 True Profitability by Quadrant of the 80/20 Matrix

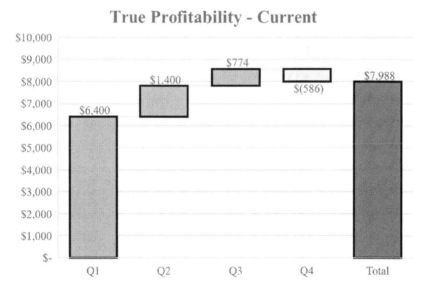

Notice how our true operating profit is being dragged down by the complexity of Q4 where we have little revenue but a dis-proportionate higher cost. As covered before in this book, a typical transformation exercise could potentially utilize several different strategies by quadrant. For Q4, it will be mostly about rationalizing and fixing the limp tail, re-pricing and phasing out SKUs, and even divesting from loss-making customers.

For Q3, it's about increasing BOM similarity levels, reducing part count, and optimizing the supply chain. We want to simplify the offering while in conjunction with our core customers. Q2 is all about lowering transactional complexity when dealing with low-volume customers. We need to single out strategic and baby-whale clients, but we also want to improve margins through pricing and differentiate terms and conditions for the twenty customers versus the eighty ones.

In Q1, the business should be looking for efficiencies in areas such as direct material cost reductions and manufacturing processes. The whole supply chain can be evaluated to identify where optimization can occur, for example, BOM similarity for tighter inventory management for high volume SKU components. Therefore, our 80/20 modeled analytics gives us an outline strategy of where to engineer a profitability improvement. The model also indicates the size of the prize, as shown below.

7.5 Sizing the "Prize" by Quadrant

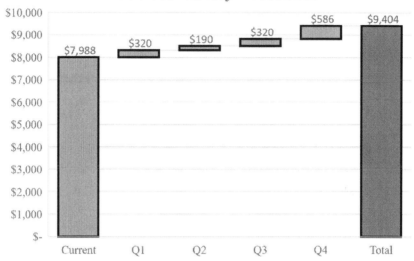

By using a dynamic model with compelling visualizations, a business can define clear objectives and drive focus on these. The precise value here is that these opportunities are not getting stuck in a data swamp or the "spreadsheet from hell." Instead, improvement strategies arise for various areas of the organization, directly from a click-and-explore live model. This one source of truth allows our XYZ business stakeholders to focus and become aligned with what is essential and track its success. A 5%+ operating profit improvement is now not only more than possible, but it has a series of concrete activities associated with reaching this outcome that is entirely within a company's capabilities and resources. The main difference is that the road map with its milestones has been defined and can be followed by all.

ABOUT THE AUTHORS

Pedro Ferro is a partner and CEO at Luzio Strategy North America. Pedro has thirty years of management experience in manufacturing and technology businesses. Before Luzio, he was CEO of Fras-le and President of Meritor's Aftermarket. He has degrees in business and mechanical and industrial engineering, having spent most of his professional life working outside of his native Brazil. Pedro has led many implementations of 80/20 throughout his career in different companies. He is the author of two other books: "The Vital Few Natural Laws" and "Lean on Steroids." Pedro resides in Charlotte, North Carolina.

Patrick Mosimann is a partner and CEO at AlignAlytics. Patrick has supported businesses across multiple industries for over twenty years, with a specialization in Pricing and Sales Growth, but also Supply Chain, Innovation, Implementing Strategic Initiatives, Segmentation, Cost to Serve, and Financial Drivers. Patrick's expertise and experience include strategy consulting experience, advanced data expertise, and broad analytics tools and software know-how. Patrick resides in London, England.

[i] https://surveys.align-alytics.com/#/true-profitability-survey

[ii] Simon Herbert: Nobel Prize in Economics (1978)

[iii] Wikipedia (https://en.wikipedia.org/wiki/Bounded_rationality): Bounded rationality is the idea that rationality is limited when individuals make decisions: by the tractability of the decision problem, the cognitive limitations of the mind, and the time available to make the decision. Decision-makers, in this view, act as satisficers, seeking a satisfactory solution rather than an optimal one. Herbert A. Simon proposed bounded rationality as an alternative basis for the mathematical modeling of decision-making, as used in economics, political science and related disciplines. It complements "rationality as optimization", which views decision-making as a fully rational process of finding an optimal choice given the information available.

[iv] Harvard Business Review - The Problem with Product Proliferation Martin Mocker and Jeanne W. Ross, from May-June 2017 issue

[v] Inbound Logistics Magazine - August 2014 - Managing SKU Proliferation in the Beverage Industry by John Deris - Senior Vice President of National Sales for Fleet Management Solutions, Ryder Systems Inc.

[vi] Coca-Cola: When less is more - Financial Times - April 20, 2015, by Neil Munshi and Scheherazade Daneshkhu

[vii] Jeffrey Towson - What to do when you fail in China - posted on May 2, 2017

[viii] The Granularity of Growth (How to Identify the Sources of Growth and Drive Enduring Company Performance) – Patrick Viguerie, Sven Smit, Mehrdad Baghai. Published by John Wiley & Sons, Inc., Hoboken, New Jersey (United States 2008

[ix] Harvard Business School - Technology and Operations Management - Digital Initiative - Written by Bravo and Posted on December 9, 2015

[x] Know Your Customers' "Jobs to Be Done" by Clayton M. Christensen, Taddy Hall, Karen Dillon, and David S. Duncan – Harvard Business Review – September 2016 Issue.

[xi] https://blog.toyota.co.uk/tnga-explained-engineering-for-the-future - April 15, 2015 and Automotive News Europe, May 2013

[xii] Market Watch 10 things that make electric-car maker Tesla special - Published: Aug 23, 2016 3:02 p.m. ET

[xiii] Business Insider - Matthew DeBord Jun. 21, 2018, 5:13 PM

[xiv] TRIZ comes from the Russian acronym "Theoria Resheneyava Isobrethatelskehuh Zadach" developed by Altshuller and others, from the former USSR, between 1946 and 1985.

[xv] Porter's Five Forces - https://www.mindtools.com/pages/article/newTMC_08.htm

[xvi] The Hidden History of Swiss Watchmaking's Biggest Rivals • Gear Patrol www. gearpatrol.com - 2019/02/12

[xvii] International Design Conference – Design 2008 – Design for Variety – Efficient Support for Design Engineers (T. Kipp and D. Krause)

[xviii] "The Spirit in the Walls: A Pattern for High Performance at Scania" - H. Thomas Johnson and Anders Broms - May/June 1995

[xviii] McCarthy, I.P. (2004). "Special issue editorial: the what, why and how of mass customization." Production Planning & Control.

[xx] ITW Business Philosophies" E-Learning Program - http://itwelearning.com/pdf_files/ITW%20Business%20Philosophies_Course%20Summaries.pdf - Retrieved on 7/5/14.

[xxi] The Four Faces of Mass Customization by James H. Gilmore and B. Joseph Pine II - Harvard Business Review - Jan/Feb - 1997 issue - https://hbr.org/1997/01/the-four-faces-of-mass-customization

[xxii] https://www.scania.com/global/en/home/products-and-services/configurator-portal.html

[xxiii] Michael Schrage – AI is Going to Change the 80/20 Rule – Harvard Business Review - Feb. 28, 2017

Made in the USA
Coppell, TX
06 December 2019